Executive Data Science

A Guide to Training and Managing the Best
Data Scientists

Brian Caffo, Roger D. Peng and
Jeffrey Leek

Executive Data Science

A Guide to Training and Managing the Best Data Scientists

Brian Caffo, Roger D. Peng and Jeffrey Leek

ISBN 978-1-365-12197-5

Leanpub

This is a Leanpub book. Leanpub empowers authors and publishers with the Lean Publishing process. Lean Publishing is the act of publishing an in-progress ebook using lightweight tools and many iterations to get reader feedback, pivot until you have the right book and build traction once you do.

Also By These Authors

Books by Brian Caffo

Statistical inference for data science

Regression Models for Data Science in R

Advanced Linear Models for Data Science

Developing Data Products in R

Books by Roger D. Peng

R Programming for Data Science

The Art of Data Science

Exploratory Data Analysis with R

Report Writing for Data Science in R

Books by Jeffrey Leek

The Elements of Data Analytic Style

How to be a modern scientist

Contents

CONTENTS

A Crash Course in Data Science

What is Data Science?

Note: Some of the material in this section appeared on the Simply Statistics Blog

Because this is a book about data science, it might be reasonable to first ask, "What is data science?". Most people hyping data science have focused on the first word: *data*. They care about volume and velocity and whatever other buzzwords describe data that is too big for you to analyze in Excel. This hype about the size (relative or absolute) of the data being collected fed into the second category of hype: hype about *tools*. People threw around EC2, Hadoop, Pig, and had huge debates about Python versus R.

But the key word in data science is not "data"; it is *science*. Data science is only useful when the data are used to answer a question. That is the science part of the equation. The problem with this view of data science is that it is much harder than the view that focuses on data size or tools. It is much easier to calculate the size of a data set and say "My data are bigger than yours" or to say, "I can code in Hadoop, can you?" than to say, "I have this really hard question, can I answer it with my data?"

A few reasons it is harder to focus on the science than the data/tools are:

- John Tukey's quote: "The combination of some data and an aching desire for an answer does not ensure that a reasonable answer can be extracted from a given body of data." You may have 100 Gb and only 3 Kb are useful for answering the real question you care about.

- When you start with the question you often discover that you need to collect new data or design an experiment to confirm you are getting the right answer.
- It is easy to discover structure or networks in a data set. There will always be correlations for a thousand reasons if you collect enough data. Understanding whether these correlations matter for specific, interesting questions is much harder.
- Often the structure you found on the first pass is due to a phenomeon (measurement error, artifacts, data processing) that isn't related to answer an interesting question.

The hype around big data/data science will flame out (it already is) if data science is only about "data" and not about science. The long term impact of data science will be measured by the scientific questions we can answer with the data.

Moneyball

One of the examples that you hear about a lot when you hear about data science is Moneyball. With Moneyball, the question was, can we build a winning baseball team if we have a really limited budget? They used quantification of player skills, and developed a new metric that's more useful to answer that question. But the key underlying question that they were asking, the key reason why this was a data science problem, was "Could we use the data that we collected to answer this specific question, which is *building a low budget baseball team?*"

Voter Turnout

A second question would be, "How do we find the people who vote for Barack Obama and make sure that those people end up at the polls on polling day?" And so this is an example from a study of Barack Obama's data team, where they went and they actually tried to run experiments and analyze the data to identify those people. They ended up being a surprising group of people that weren't necessarily the moderate voters that everybody thought they would be, that could be swayed to go out and vote for Barack Obama.

This is again an example where there was a high-level technical issue that had been used–A/B testing on websites and things like that–to collect and identify the data that they used to answer the question. But at the core, the data science question was "Can we use data to answer this question about voter turnout, to make sure a particular candidate wins an election.

Engineering Solutions

We've talked a lot about how data science is about answering questions with data. While that's definitely true there are also some other components to the problem. Data science is involved in formulating quantitative questions, identifying the data that could be used to answer those questions, cleaning it, making it nice, then analyzing the data, whether that's with machine learning, or with statistics, or with the latest neural network approaches. The final step involves communicating that answer to other people.

One component of this entire process that often gets left out in these discussions is the engineering component of it.n A good example of where the engineering component is critical came up with the Netflix prize. With the Netflix prize, Netflix had a whole bunch of teams competing to try to predict how best to show people what movies to watch next. The team that won blended together a large number of machine learning algorithms. But it turns out that's really computationally hard to do, and so Netflix never actually ended up implementing the winning solution on their system, because there wasn't enough computing power to do that at a scale where they could do it for all their customers.

In addition to the actual data science, the actual learning from data and discovering what the right prediction model is, there's the implementation component (often lumped into data engineering) which is how you actually implement or scale that technology to be able to apply it to, say, a large customer base or to a large number of people all at once.

There are trade-offs that always come up in data science. The trade-offs between interpretability and accuracy or interpretability and speed, or interpretability and scalability, and so forth. You can imagine that there are all these different components to a model: whether it's interpretable, simple, accurate, fast, and scalable. You have to make judgments about which of those things are important for the particular problem that you're trying to solve.

What is Statistics Good For?

Get the lecture notes used in the videos.

Statistics is the discipline of analyzing data. As such it intersects heavily with data science, machine learning and, of course, traditional statistical analysis. In this section, we orient you to statistics by covering a few key activities that define the field. These are:

- Descriptive statistics
- Inference
- Prediction
- Experimental Design

Descriptive statistics includes exploratory data analysis, unsupervised learning, clustering and basic data summaries. Descriptive statistics have many uses, most notably helping us get familiar with a data set. Descriptive statistics usually are the starting point for any analysis. Often, descriptive statistics help us arrive at hypotheses to be tested later with more formal inference.

Inference is the process of making conclusions about populations from samples. Inference includes most of the activities traditionally associated with statistics such as: estimation, confidence intervals, hypothesis tests and variability. Inference forces us to formally define targets of estimations or hypotheses. It forces us to think about the population that we're trying to generalize to from our sample.

Prediction overlaps quite a bit with inference, but modern prediction tends to have a different mindset. Prediction is the process of trying to guess an outcome given a set of realizations of the outcome and some predictors. Machine learning, regression, deep learning, boosting, random forests and logistic regression are all prediction algorithms. If the target of prediction is binary or categorical, prediction is often called classification. In modern prediction, emphasis shifts from building small, parsimonious, interpretable models to focusing on prediction performance, often estimated via cross validation. Generalizability is often given not by a sampling model, as in traditional inference, but by challenging the algorithm on novel datasets. Prediction has transformed many fields include e-commerce, marketing and financial forecasting.

Experimental design is the act of controlling your experimental process to optimize the chance of arriving at sound conclusions. The most notable example of experimental design is randomization. In randomization a treatment is randomized across experimental units to make treatment groups as comparable as possible. Clinical trials and A/B testing both employ randomization. In random sampling, one tries to randomly sample from a population of interest to get better generalizability of the results to the population. Many election polls try to get a random sample.

What is Machine Learning?

The lecture notes used for this section.

Machine learning has been a revolution in modern prediction and clustering. Machine learning has become an expansive field involving computer science, statistics and engineering. Some of the algorithms have their roots in artificial intelligence (like neural networks and deep learning).

For data scientists, we decompose two main activities of machine learning. (Of course, this list is non-exhaustive.) These are are

1. **Unsupervised learning** - trying to uncover unobserved factors in the data. It is called "unsupervised" as there is no gold standard outcome to judge against. Some example algorithms including hierarchical clustering, principal components analysis, factor analysis and k-means.
2. **Supervised learning** - using a collection of predictors, and some observed outcomes, to build an algorithm to predict the outcome when it is not observed. Some examples include: neural networks, random forests, boosting and support vector machines.

One famous early example of unsupervised clustering in the computation of the g-factor. This was postulated to be a measure of intrinsic intelligence. Early factor analytic models were used to cluster scores on psychometric questions to create the g-factor. Notice the lack of a gold standard outcome. There was no true measure of intrinsic intelligence to train an algorithm to predict it.

For supervised learning, an early example is the development of regression. In this, Francis Galton wanted to predict children's heights from their parents. He developed linear regression in the process. Notice that having several children with known adult heights along with their parents allows one to build the model, then apply it to parents who are expecting.

It is worth contrasting modern machine learning and prediction with more traditional statistics. Traditional statistics has a great deal of overlap with machine learning, including models that produce very good predictions and methods for clustering. However, there is much more of an emphasis in traditional statistics on modeling and inference, the problem of extending results to a population. Modern machine learning was somewhat of a revolution in statistics not only because of the performance of the algorithms for supervised and unsupervised problems, but also from a paradigm shift away from a focus on models and inference. Below we characterize some of these differences.

For this discussion, I would summarize (focusing on supervised learning) some characteristics of ML as:

- the emphasis on predictions;
- evaluating results via prediction performance;
- having concern for overfitting but not model complexity per se;
- emphasis on performance;
- obtaining generalizability through performance on novel datasets;
- usually no superpopulation model specified;
- concern over performance and robustness.

In contrast, I would characterize the typical characteristics of traditional statistics as:

- emphasizing superpopulation inference;
- focusing on a-priori hypotheses;
- preferring simpler models over complex ones (parsimony), even if the more complex models perform slightly better;
- emphasizing parameter interpretability;
- having statistical modeling or sampling assumptions that connect data to a population of interest;
- having concern over assumptions and robustness.

In recent years, the distinction between both fields have substantially faded. ML researchers have worked tirelessly to improve interpretations while statistical researchers have improved the prediction performance of their algorithms.

What is Software Engineering for Data Science?

Software is the generalization of a specific aspect of a data analysis. If specific parts of a data analysis require implementing or applying a number of procedures or tools together, software is the encompassing of all these tools into a specific module or procedure that can be repeatedly applied in a variety of settings. Software allows for the systematizing and the standardizing of a procedure, so that different people can use it and understand what it's going to do at any given time.

Software is useful because it formalizes and abstracts the functionality of a set of procedures or tools, by developing a well defined interface to the analysis. Software will have an interface, or a set of inputs and a set of outputs that are well understood. People can think about the inputs and the outputs without having to worry about the gory details of what's going on underneath. Now, they may be interested in those details, but the application of the software at any given setting will not necessarily depend on the knowledge of those details. Rather, the knowledge of the *interface* to that software is important to using it in any given situation.

For example, most statistical packages will have a linear regression function which has a very well defined interface. Typically, you'll have to input things like the outcome and the set of predictors, and maybe there will be some other inputs like the data set or weights. Most linear regression

13

functions kind of work in that way. And importantly, the user does not have to know exactly how the linear regression calculation is done underneath the hood. Rather, they only need to know that they need to specify the outcome, the predictors, and a couple of other things. The linear regression function abstracts all the details that are required to implement linear regression, so that the user can apply the tool in a variety of settings.

There are three levels of software that are important to consider, going from kind of the simplest to the most abstract.

1. At the first level you might just have some code that you wrote, and you might want to encapsulate the automation of a set of procedures using a loop (or something similar) that repeats an operation multiple times.

2. The next step might be some sort of function. Regardless of what language you may be using, often there will be some notion of a function, which is used to encapsulate a set of instructions. And the key thing about a function is that you'll have to define some sort of interface, which will be the inputs to the function. The function may also have a set of outputs or it may have some side effect for example, if it's a plotting function. Now the user only needs to know those inputs and what the outputs will be. This is the first level of abstraction that you might encounter, where you have to actually define and interface to that function.

3. The highest level is an actual software package, which will often be a collection of functions and other things. That will be a little bit more formal because there'll be a very specific interface or API that a user has to understand. Often for a software package there'll be a number of convenience features for users, like

documentation, examples, or tutorials that may come with it, to help the user apply the software to many different settings. A full on software package will be most general in the sense that it should be applicable to more than one setting.

One question that you'll find yourself asking, is at what point do you need to systematize common tasks and procedures across projects versus recreating code or writing new code from scratch on every new project? It depends on a variety of factors and answering this question may require communication within your team, and with people outside of your team. You may need to develop an understanding of how often a given process is repeated, or how often a given type of data analysis is done, in order to weigh the costs and benefits of investing in developing a software package or something similar.

Within your team, you may want to ask yourself, "Is the data analysis you're going to do something that you are going to build upon for future work, or is it just going to be a one shot deal?" In our experience, there are relatively few one shot deals out there. Often you will have to do a certain analysis more than once, twice, or even three times, at which point you've reached the threshold where you want to write some code, write some software, or at least a function. The point at which you need to systematize a given set of procedures is going to be sooner than you think it is. The initial investment for developing more formal software will be higher, of course, but that will likely pay off in time savings down the road.

A basic rule of thumb is

- If you're going to do something **once** (that does happen on occasion), just write some code and document it very well. The important thing is that you want to make sure that you understand what the code does, and so that requires both writing the code well and writing documentation. You want to be able to reproduce it down later on if you ever come back to it, or if someone else comes back to it.

- If you're going to do something **twice**, write a function. This allows you to abstract a small piece of code, and it forces you to define an interface, so you have well defined inputs and outputs.

- If you're going to do something **three** times or more, you should think about writing a small package. It doesn't have to be commercial level software, but a small package which encapsulates the set of operations that you're going to be doing in a given analysis. It's also important to write some real documentation so that people can understand what's supposed to be going on, and can apply the software to a different situation if they have to.

Structure of a Data Science Project

A typical data science project will be structured in a few different phases. There's roughly five different phases that we can think about in a data science project.

The first phase is the most important phase, and that's the phase where you ask the question and you specify what is it that you're interested in learning from data. Now, specifying the question and kind of refining it over time is really important because it will ultimately guide the data that you obtain and the type of analysis that you do. Part of specifying the question is also determining the type of question that you are gonna be asking. There are six types of questions that you can ask going from kind of descriptive, to exploratory, to inferential, to causal, to prediction, predictive and mechanistic. And so figuring out what type of question you're asking and what exactly is the type of question is really influential. You should spend a lot of time thinking about this.

Once you've kind of figured out what your question is, but typically you'll get some data. Now, either you'll have the data or you'll have to go out and get it somewhere or maybe someone will provide it to you, but the data will come to you. The the next phase will be exploratory data analysis. So this is the second part, there are two main goals to exploratory data analysis. The first is you want to know *if the data that you have is suitable for answering the question that you have.* This will depend on a variety of questions ranging from basic ones—"Is there enough data?", "Are there too many missing values?"—to more fundamental ones, like are you missing certain variables or do you need to collect more data to get those variables, etc?

The second goal of exploratory data analysis is to start to develop a sketch of the solution. If the data are appropriate for answering your question, you can start using it to sketch out what the answer might be to get a sense of what it might look like. This can be done without any formal modeling or any kind of the statistical testing.

The next stage, the third stage, is formal modeling. If your sketch seems to work, you've got the right data and it seems appropriate to move on, the formal modeling phase is the way to specifically write down what questions you're asking and to lay out what parameters you're trying to estimate. It also provides a framework for challenging your results. Just because you've come up with an answer in the exploratory data analysis phase doesn't mean that it's necessarily going to be the right answer and you need to be able to challenge your results to examine their sensitivity to different assumptions. Challenging your model and developing a formal framework is really important to making sure that you can develop robust evidence for answering your question.

Once you've done your analysis and your formal modeling you want to think about how to interpret your results. There are a variety of things to think about in the interpretation phase the data science project. The first is to think about how your results comport with what you expected to find when you where first asking the question (before you had data). You also want to think about totality of the evidence that you've developed. You've probably done many different analyses, you probably fit many different models. And so you have many different bits of information to think about. Part of the challenge of the interpretation phase is to assemble all of the information and weigh each of the different pieces of evidence. You know which pieces are more reliable, which are are more uncertain than others, and which more important than others to get a sense of the totality of evidence with respect to answering the question.

The last phase is the communication phase. Any data science project that is successful will want to communicate its findings to some sort of audience. That audience may be internal to your organization, it may be external, it may be to a large audience or even just a few people. But communicating your findings is an essential part of data science because it informs the data analysis process and a it translates your findings into action.

So that's the last part (which is not necessarily a formal part of a data science project)—often there will be some *decision* that needs to be made or some action that needs to be taken. And the data science project will have been conducted in support of making a decision or taking an action. That last phase will depend on more than just the results of the data analysis, but may require inputs from many different parts of an organization or from other stakeholders. Ultimately if a decision is made, the data analysis will inform that decision and the evidence that was collected will support that decision.

To summarize, the five phases of a data science project are

1. Question
2. Exploratory data analysis
3. Formal modeling
4. Interpretation
5. Communication.

Now, there is another approach that can be taken, it's very often taken in a data science project. This approach starts with the data and an exploratory data analysis. Often there will be a data set already available, but it won't be immediately clear what the data set will be useful for. So it can be useful to do some exploratory data analysis, to look at the data, to summarize it a little bit, make some plots, and see what's there. This process can you lead you to generate interesting questions based on the data. This process is sometimes called hypothesis generating because the goal is to produce questions as opposed to answers. Once you've produced the questions that you want to ask it may be useful to get more data or other data to do an exploratory data analysis that's more specific to your question. After that, you can continue with the formal modeling, interpretation and communication.

One thing that you have to be wary of is to do the exploratory data analysis in one data set, develop the question, and then go back to the *same* data set, pretending like you hadn't done the exploratory data analysis before. This is often be a recipe for bias in your analysis because the results were derived from the same dataset that was used to generate the question. It's important to be careful about not doing that and to always try to obtain other independent data when you're using the data to generate the questions in the first place. That said, this approach to data science can be very useful and can often result in many interesting questions.

Output of a Data Science Experiment

The lecture notes can be found here.

The potential set of outputs of a data science experiment are pretty much limitless. However, four general types of outputs pop up most frequently. Those are:

- Reports
- Presentations
- Interactive web pages
- Apps

(Interactive graphics are important enough to merit their own category. However, they're usually embedded in a web page, so I'm lumping them in there.) Let's discuss each of the categories in turn.

Reports are easily the most common output of a data science experiment. Since the goals of reports varies wildly across settings, let's simply discuss a few hallmarks of a good data science report. It should:

- Be clearly written
- Involve a narrative around the data
- Discuss the creation of the analytic dataset
- Have concise conclusions
- Omit unnecessary details
- Be reproducible

By and large, these points are obvious. However, this latter point is one that we discuss a lot throughout the specialization. Reproducible reports have mechanisms under the hood to recreate the data analysis. The number of benefits of report writing in this fashion are many. They include: getting the data scientist to think about the output of the process (since the code is embedded in the eventual output), very clear documentation that extends beyond code commenting, automation of the report generation process and then, of course, reproducibility. The main tools for producing reproducible reports are kntir and ipython notebooks. You should create a culture of using these tools, or similar ones, in your organization, as they will dramatically improve reproducibility.

Oddly enough, the same rules apply to presentations, though reproducible presentation software is less well adopted. For R, there's slidify and rStudio's presenter. These tools automate presentations in the same way that knitr and ipython notebooks automate report generation.

Interactive web pages and apps are similar enough to combined in the discussion. Again, as the requirements will vary so much across applications, we will only discuss a few hallmarks of good output. These include:

- Good ease of use / design
- Good documentation
- Code commented
- Code version controlled

Good ease of use and design are a discipline unto themselves. Since your data scientists are likely also not software engineers or designers, their design is probably not going to be optimal. However, modern tools allow data scientists to prototype apps and interactive web pages quickly and relatively easily. Your data scientists should then pay some attention to ease use and design. Good documentation is mostly effort, though the same caveats apply with design.

On the other hand, having well commented code and version control should be standard practice for data scientists. Well commented code is easy to return to for new employees or the original coder returning to the project after a long hiatus. Version control is similar good practice. With version control, data scientists will be able to return to any checked in version of the project. The comments are useful for documenting the evolution of the project as well. Tools such as git and github make version control easy and are in the standard toolkit of data scientists.

Defining Success: Four Secrets of a Successful Data Science Experiment

Here's a link to the lecture notes.

Defining success is a crucial part of managing a data science experiment. Of course, success is often context specific. However, some aspects of success are general enough to merit discussion. My list of hallmarks of success includes:

1. New knowledge is created.
2. Decisions or policies are made based on the outcome of the experiment.
3. A report, presentation or app with impact is created.
4. It is learned that the data can't answer the question being asked of it.

Some more negative outcomes include: decisions being made that disregard clear evidence from the data, equivocal results that do not shed light in one direction or another, uncertainty prevents new knowledge from being created.

Let's discuss some of the successful outcomes first.

New knowledge seems ideal to me (especially since I'm an academic). However, new knowledge doesn't necessarily mean that it's important. If it produces actionable decisions or policies, that's even better. (Wouldn't it be great if there was an evidence-based policy like the evidence-based medicine movement that has transformed medicine.) That

25

our data science products have great (positive) impact is of course ideal. Creating reusable code or apps is great way to increase the impact of a project.

Finally, the last point is perhaps the most controversial. I view it as a success if we can show that the data can't answer the questions being asked. I am reminded of a friend who told a story of the company he worked at. They hired many expensive prediction consultants to help use their data to inform pricing. However, the prediction results weren't helping. They were able to prove that the data couldn't answer the hypothesis under study. There was too much noise and the measurements just weren't accurately measuring what was needed. Sure, the result wasn't optimal, as they still needed to know how to price things, but it did save money on consultants. I have since heard this story repeated nearly identically by friends in different industries.

Data Science Toolbox

The data scientist toolbox is the collection of tools that are used to store, process, analyze and communicate results of data science experiments. Data are typically stored in a database. For a smaller organization that might be single, small MySQL database. And for a large organization, it might be a large distributed database across many servers. Usually, most of the analysis that takes place and most of the production doesn't actually happen in the database—it happens elsewhere. You usually have to use another programming language to pull the data out of that database to analyze it.

There are two common languages for analyzing data. The first one is the R programming language. R is a statistical programming language that allows you to pull data out of a database, analyze it, and produce visualizations very quickly. The other major programming language that's used for this type of analysis is Python. Python is another similar language that allows you to pull data out of databases, analyze and manipulate it, visualize it, and connected to downstream production.

The other thing that you need to do to be able to use these languages is some kind of computing infrastructure that you can use to run those programming languages on. You have the database, which stores the data, and then you have the servers which you will use to analyze the data. One useful example is Amazon Web Services. This is a set of computing resources that you can actually rent from Amazon, so many organizations that do data analysis actually just directly rent their computing resources rather than buy and manage their own. This is particularly true for small organizations that don't have a large IT budget.

Once you've actually done some low-level analysis and maybe made some discoveries or done some experiments, and decided actually how you're going to use data to make decisions for your organization you might want to scale those solutions up. There's a large number of analysis tools that can be used to provide more scalable analyses of datasets, whether that's in a database or by pulling the data out of the database. So two of the most popular right now are the Hadoop framework and the Spark framework. And both of these are basically ways to analyze, at a very large scale, data sets. Now it is possible to do interactive analysis with both of these, particularly with Spark. But it's a little bit more complicated and little bit more expensive, especially if you're applying it to large sets of data. Therefore, it's very typical in the data science process to take the database, pull out a small sample of the data, process it and analyse it in R or Python and then go back to the engineering team and scale it back up with Hadoop, or Spark, or other tools like that.

The next tool in the data scientist toolbox is actually communication. A data scientist or a data engineer has a job that's typically changing quite rapidly as new packages and new sort of tools become available, and so the quickest way to keep them up to speed is to have quick communication and to have an open channel of communication. A lot of data science teams use tools like Slack to communicate with each other, to basically be able to post new results, new ideas, and be able to communicate about what the latest packages are available.

There are a large number of help websites like Stack Overflow, that allow people go out and search for the questions that they need to answer. Even if they're quite technical, and quite detailed, it's possible to get answers relatively quickly. And that allows people to keep the process moving, even though the technology is changing quite rapidly.

Once the analysis is done and you want to share it with other people in your organization, you need to do that with reproducible or literate documentation. What does that mean? It basically means a way to integrate the analysis code and the figures and the plots that have been created by the data scientist with plain text that can be used to explain what's going on. One example is the R Markdown framework. Another example is iPython notebooks. These are ways to make your analysis reproducible and make it possible that if one data scientist runs an analysis and they want to hand it off to someone else, they'll be able to easily do that.

You also need to be able to visualize the results of the data science experiment. So the end product is often some kind of data visualization or interactive data experience. There are a large number of tools that are available to build those sorts of interactive experiences and visualizations because at the end user of a data science product is very often not a data scientist themselves. It's often a manager or an executive who needs to handle that data, understand what's happening with it, and make a decision. One such tool is Shiny, which is a way to build data products that you can share with people who don't necessarily have a lot of data science experience.

Finally, most of the time when you do a science data experiment, you don't do it in isolation—you want to communicate your results to other people. People frequently make data presentations, whether that's the data science manager, the data engineer, or the data scientist themselves, that explains how they actually performed that data science experiment. What are the techniques that they used, what are the caveats, and how can their analysis be applied to the data to make a decision.

Separating Hype from Value

You've probably heard a lot about data science and big data. Frankly, there's been a lot of hype around these areas. What that's done is it has inflated expectations about what data science and data can actually accomplish. Overall that has been a net negative for the field of data science and for big data. It's useful to think for just a bit about what are the questions you can ask to separate *data science hype* from *data science hope*.

The first question is always "What is the question you are trying to answer with the data?" If someone comes to talk to you about a big data project, or a data science project, and they start talking about the hottest new cool technology they can use to do distributed computing, and analyze data with machine learning and they throw a bunch of buzz words at you, the very first question you should ask is "What is the question you're trying to answer with data?" Because that really narrows the question down and it filters out a lot of the hype around what tools and technologies people are using which can often be very interesting and fun to talk about. We like to talk about them too, but they're not really going to add value to your organization all by themselves.

The second question to ask is, once you've identified what that question is you're trying to answer with the data, is "Do you have the data to actually answer that question?" So often the question that you want to answer and the data that you have to answer it with are not actually very compatible with each other. And so you have to ask yourself "Can we get the data in a shape where we can actually answer the question we want to answer?" Sometimes the answer is just no, in which case, you have to give up (for now). Bottom line—if you want to decide on whether a project is hype or whether it's reality, you need to decide whether the data the people are trying to use are actually relevant for the question they are trying to answer.

The third thing you need to ask is "If you could answer the question with the data you have, could you even use the answer in a meaningful way?" This question goes back to that idea from the Netflix prize where there was a solution to the problem of predicting which videos people would like to watch. And it was a very very good solution but it wasn't a solution that could be implemented with the computing resources that Netflix had in a way that was financially expedient. Even though they could answer the question, even though they did have the right data, even though they were answering a specific question, they couldn't actually apply the results of what they figured out.

If you ask these three questions, you can very quickly decipher whether a data science project is about hype or whether it's about a real contribution that can really move your organisation forward.

Building the Data Science Team

The Data Team

The first thing to know when building a data science organization is that data science is a team sport. It takes a large group of people working together to solve real, practical data science projects. Those people include the data scientists, the managers of those data scientists, and data engineers who perform and develop the infrastructure. There are also people who your team will have contact with outside of the data science team.

The data science team members work together as a unit. Often, each of these people is working on an individual project, or a sub-problem of a larger data science problem. And then they come together and have joint group meetings and joint presentations, where they discuss their ideas. They also interact with external folks either directly through individual meetings with people outside of the data science team or through the data science manager. Either way, they have to be able to communicate what's going on with the data science infrastructure and what's going on with the data science team.

When Do You Need Data Science?

The way in which you'll interact with data science depends a little bit on what kind of organization you are. To some extent, it depends a lot on the size of your organization.

The Startup

When you're just a start up, at an early stage company, or you're just one person with a very small team you may not need to worry so much about how to do experimentation, how to do machine learning, how to do prediction and downstream calculations. The first order of business is just making sure your data house is in order. The way to do that is to make sure you focus on infrastructure.

The first thing that you need to do is build out the infrastructure for storing the data, the databases and so forth. The software that's going to be run to pull those data, the servers that are going to serve the data to other people, and the servers that you'll interact with yourself in order to get the data out. All of that requires infrastructure building. So often the first people that you get to hire into a data science team are not people that you would necessarily called data scientists in the sense that they're not analyzing the data, they're not doing machine learning. They might do a little bit of that but mostly they're involved on just making sure the machine is running, making sure the data's getting collected, it's secure, it's stored and so forth.

The Mid-Sized Organization

When you're a mid-size organization, then hopefully you've got the basic infrastructure in place and you can start thinking about building out your real data science team. To do that you can bring on board people that are actually called data scientists and those are the folks who will then actually use the data. They might run some experiments. They might build machine learning algorithms. They might analyze the data to see if you can identify any patterns or trends in behavior that you care about. So at that point, you're thinking about actually building out the data science team. You're also thinking about implementing these data science ideas and products.

For example, the data scientist might build something like a machine learning algorithm that predicts consumer behavior. Once you have that algorithm built out, you might need to implement it back on to your system. And you might need to scale it up, so that it can be run on the whole data set. You might want to build some sort of visualization, that people who aren't necessarily data scientists can interact with. And so, that would be turning it back over to the data engineering team. That means there are still infrastructure concerns, because you have a large set of data that you've hopefully collected at this point. You need to be secure about it, you need to have a database, you need to be able to scale it. But, now you're sort of graduating into a more complete view of data science.

Large Organizations

For a large organization you have all those same sorts of things. You now have a data infrastructure, you might have a data science team that's running experiments. You may be using those experiments to make decisions. But now you have one additional component, which is really managing the team and keeping everybody on task and coordinated. So at this point the data science manager role becomes a little bit more involved, in the sense that you might be coordinating multiple teams of data scientists working on different projects. You might have a team that works exclusively on building machine learning projects. You might have another team that works exclusively on running experiments and inferring what you can from those experiments.

Someone has to be in charge of coordinating those activities making sure they're connected to the right people within your organization. Whether that's the marketing team, the business group or whoever else that you're collaborating with. You have to be able to connect those people and so at that scale the full data science infrastructure is in place.

Qualifications & Skills

Data Engineer

One of the key members of a data science team is a data engineer. What does a data engineer do? They might do things like build infrastructure, so they would build out your databases and the hardware for that. That might involve purchasing equipment and organizing it within your organization. Or they might build out your system for actually computing on that infrastructure, whether it's what servers they're going to buy and how they're going to organize that. And what software they're going to run on top of the database, what software they're going to run on top of the server. They might manage the data storage and use and they might monitor how those work. They might monitor what people are using which data. They might pull data out and give it to somebody. And then they might implement production tools.

Now each of these is a different thing, and so you might not have one person that does all of these things. Certainly at the beginning, when you're a very small organization, you might need one person that can kind of handle the entire data infrastructure. Then you might get more specialized people as you get to be a larger and larger organization.

The question is, what skills do they need? They might need some knowledge of what's the right hardware to be looking for, both in terms of storage and in terms of computing. They need to have some knowledge about database software and they need to know a little bit about software for computing and what are the different software needs that your organization might have. In that sense, they need to be able to interact with the data scientists, once you have them.

They need to be able to know what software they need to be able to install, what kind of data pulls that people will frequently do. That will inform the hardware choices that they're going to be making. They also need to understand data processing at scale because almost always now organizations are collecting a massive amount of data. You need to be able to run at scale those data processes and those data prediction algorithms that you've developed. Data engineers need to understand software engineering to the point where they know how they're going to interact with all these other components of the data science team.

The background for data engineers is often computer science and computer engineering, but they could also come from other places. They might come from a quantitative background with some computer science experience that they picked up maybe in online courses or in courses in person. Or maybe they come from information technology where they've actually been involved in infrastructure building and so forth. Not unlike with the data scientist, you might depend on what your organization needs a little bit, which of these specific backgrounds is most useful to you. But the primary thing you want to know is Can they execute those jobs that your organization needs them to execute? Are they able to build infrastructure? Are they able to maintain the infrastructure that you need them to be able to maintain? Can they implement the data science, or machine learning algorithms, or statistical experiments, at scale for your organization in the way that you would like them to?

The key is to get them to be able to solve the problems that you need now. With a data engineer, the balance of solutions versus software might be a little bit different then a data scientist. Since this person is the person that's going to sort of be maintaining the data stack for you, you need them to be able to do that in a way that's consistent with the way that your organization does things. So they need to be able to have an idea about what are the specific software and hardware needs that your organization has.

There are a few key things that they need to know. They might need to know how to build and manage some databases, things like SQL, things like MongoDB. They might also need to know how to do things like implement or run things like Hadoop, which is a parallel processing infrastructure. Now it's not necessarily true that they need to know any one of these buzzwords or another. But it is true that they need to have the combination of skills that allows them to build out a data infrastructure that's supportive and that can be maintained.

There are a couple of key characteristics that you're looking for when you're looking for a data engineer. First, they need to be willing to find answers on their own. This is again, a person that often will be one of the few people that's solely responsible for the data infrastructure. Often they need be able to answer those questions themselves. They need to be able to go out and get the quotes on the Internet. They need to be able to ask questions and figure out what's the right hardware, and what are the right security measures to be taking, and so forth. Often they will have to do that a little bit on their own, in the sense that, the data engineering team is ofte very specific and expert in an area. Where it's not clear that other people within your organization will be able to give them a lot of advice. They need to know a little bit of data science. They need to know how data is used, how it's pulled, how it's analyzed. So that they know how to build the infrastructure that's useful for them. Ideally, they'll be closely collaborative with the data scientists (maybe they've done that before). And then they need to be able to work well under pressure. One reason for that is that the data infrastructure for an organization is often very critical. And if it goes down then your website might go down, or you won't be able to do any analysis, or the organization sort of grinds to a halt. Having a data engineer that's able to work well under pressure, that's able to keep things up and running, and keep things maintaining, that makes good decisions about software maintainability, and hardware maintainability, is somebody that's critical for your data engineering team.

They need to be able to interact with people. Personal communication skills are highly undervalued but are very, very important. There's going to be a lot of steps at which a data engineer is going to have to interact, especially at first in a small organization but even later on, with data scientists, with other people in your organization, and external units. And so you need to be able to have a friendly conversation with them. Ideally, they can explain in very simple terms why they need to make certain decisions. Often, the decisions are quite technical, and quite involved with the hardware and software. And so it's very useful if they can, in very simple language, explain what's going on, what the problem is, how it's going to be fixed, and so forth. That can be a huge advantage to your organization.

Data Scientist

When you're building out your data science team, one of the key roles that you'll be hiring for, no surprise, is a data scientist. This section talks a little bit about what to look for in a data scientist.

What does a data scientist do? As it's typically defined, a data scientist runs experiments, pulls and cleans data, analyzes it and then communicates the results to people. So they have to have a set of skills that allows them to perform all of these activities. Depending on your definition of data science, you might have to move the qualifications just a little bit in one direction or another. It also depends a little bit how mature your organization is. If you're hiring dedicated data scientists, then the description above likely similar to their job description. If you're at a very early stage and you're hiring your first data science team members, they might have to be a little bit more of a jack of all trades. They might need to be able to do a little bit more data engineering, as well as data science. The description corresponds more to a more mature organization that is hiring data scientists.

A data scientist needs to be able to do statistics. Often they'll have learned that either in classes, so that they will have a qualification in statistics, whether it's a degree or they've taken a large number of classes, or they've taken some online classes. They probably need to know something about prediction and machine learning. That can often be learned from either statistics classes or from computer science classes that focus on machine learning. Again, you can also learn that online.

Key areas that are covered by these topics are inference and prediction, which we've discussed in other chapters. It's important to know that some people will likely be better at one than another and it depends on what your organization is focused on doing. If you're doing more development of predictive tools, they might need to be a little stronger in machine learning. If you're trying to do experiments and come up with new hypotheses or inferences about what is effective, they might need to be a little bit better at inference.

A data scientist also needs to be able to do data analysis, and that means the whole picture: they need to be able to pull data sets out of a database, they need to be able to clean them up and analyze datasets. Perform the statistical inference or prediction that they want to do and then communicate those results. Data communication skills involve both being able to analyze the data, create nice visualizations, communicate those visualizations and the results to people in a way that both expresses what's going on and carefully expresses how uncertain they are. When you're making decisions, you know exactly how strongly the data are supporting the decision that you're trying to make.

In addition to the skills described above, data scientists usually have a few of the following skills. They usually know how to use R or Python, which are general purpose data science languages that people use to analyze data. They know how to do some kind of visualization, often interactive visualization with something like D3.js. And they'll likely know SQL in order to pull data out of a relational database.

The common backgrounds for data scientists are that they come from a statistics or biostatistics department, they learned a lot of applications, so they've actually worked on lots of real data sets. That's not always true in statistics and biostatistics department, but it's usually true for applied statistics and biostatistics departments. And then they've picked up a little bit of software engineering they know a little bit about version control they know a little bit about programming in other languages and so those sorts of things allow them to sort of interface with the other people in your company but they're primarily focused in training and statistics.

Another very common route to data science is if you do

some kind of quantitative background say for example physics or engineering, and then there's some sort of data science transition. So they either take some classes online, like our data science specialization, or they take some other data science program.

The last category that's very common among data scientists is that they've actually trained in software engineering. They're actually a trained software engineer, or a working software engineer, and they just pick up some statistics. Now, they might pick that up, again, from classes online, or they might have taken some courses in college. And again, it'll depend on the mix of what your organization is looking for. Are they looking for a person that's going to do more infrastructure development blended with a little bit of statistics? Then it might be better to go for somebody with a software engineering plus statistics background. If you already have an organization, you really need to be able to do experiments and make inferences from them. Going after somebody from a biostatistics department, for example, might be a much stronger place to go and look for your candidate.

One thing to keep in mind is that a key component of being a good data scientist is not being intimidated by new kinds of ideas or software. In some cases it's really important that you look for somebody that has specific software engineering skills, or specific programming language and skills that your organization needs. But you'll often miss out on really strong candidates by doing that. And so, one really good idea is to assess in general, are they a go getter? Are they able to learn new things? Are they able to do the sort of general purpose data science tasks that you want? And then try to figure out if they'd be able to pick up on the fly the languages that you would need them to use for your particular problem.

The key here is tp focus on the problem not on the software programming languages when you're looking for data scientists, because you'll tend to miss a huge swath of people, particularly right now in the transition while the field of data science is relatively new and there's not a standardized curriculum for training data scientists across all these different disciplines.

One of the key characteristics of data scientists that you want to have is the ability to collaborate with people to figure out what the right problem to solve is. And so they need to be able to chase that down on their own. You can't always be holding their hand. So what can you do? You can go look for evidence of this skill, whether that's through leadership that they've taken on at their previous organizations, through active participation in open source software, or whether it's through blogging, or something else where they communicate that they've gone out and they've actually been willing to go get the answers on their own. They need to be unintimidated by new data.

A smart question that often gets asked when interviewing a data scientist, is to throw out a kind of data that they've never seen before, whether it's from your organization or even data that you might have just imagined from a different organization, and see how they react to it. If they react in a way that's positive, they have ideas, they think about ways to try to tackle that problem, that's great. If they're intimidated by that data type and they're just trying to force it back into the box of the data they know, that might be very challenging as your organization changes and the data science changes for them.

In addition, it's important for a data scientist to be willing to say, I don't know. This is often hard to get out of a person in an interview, but it's important to know. If they don't know the answer to a question, because maybe you asked them a question about your organization that's very specific hat they wouldn't know the answer to, you need to see if they're comfortable saying, "I don't know," because often data come to no conclusion. It's very common for you to do an experiment and the conclusion is, we don't know very much more than we knew before we started. It's frustrating, and it's one of the hard parts about data science. But is important to know that people will, when faced with that situation, are comfortable saying "I don't know," so that you know that they'll be communicating the truth to you.

Data science requires a lot of dedication to getting all the details right, to making sure that you interact with people in a way that moves things forward, even when they're faced with not necessarily the most friendly response in return. And so it's useful if a person is very friendly, with good people skills. Those soft skills that come with being a data scientist are critical in a data science team where they're going to be working with other people and they'll often be your point of contact with external units. It's actually a grossly under valued skill in a data scientist. In our experience, people overvalue the technical component, like "Do they know programming language X?" and de-value things like, "Can they have a conversation with me that doesn't get testy if I'm questioning some of their deep-held beliefs about data?" And so, this is an important component to making sure that they'll fit in well with your organization

Data Science Manager

The last member of the data science team is a data science manager. A data science manager is responsible for building the data science team. They are responsible for identifying and recruiting data engineers and data scientists to the team; then getting them set up, setting goals and priorities, identifying those problems within an organization that need to be solved by data science, and putting the right people on the right problem. From there, they manage the data science process.

Data science, as we'll discuss in another part of this book, is a process that's not just one time, one thing. It's an *iterative process*, and so it needs to be managed carefully. One of the manager's responsibilities is making sure that people routinely interact with each other within the data science team, and also interact with other people in the wider organization. The data science team also interacts with other groups, so the manager might report to higher managers. The manager might also just interact with, or collaborate with people at their same level and other units of your organization, and so they need to have good communication skills in that sense.

What kind of skills does a data science manager need? Ideally they have knowledge of the software and hardware being used. That's great if they have some kind of background in either data science or data engineering. That's sort of the ideal case. That's ideal, because then they actually know the infrastructure that's involved. If there's a problem that comes up they might have a good suggestion about how to fix the data science infrastructure, or how to fix that machine learning algorithm that doesn't necessarily work exactly like the person wanted. They don't have to have that qualification, but it's nice.

The manager does need to know the roles in the team. They need to know what a data scientist does, what a data engineer does, what other teams are supposed to be doing, and how that may or may not be data science. They need to filter out the problems that aren't necessarily appropriate, and focus on the ones that are. They need to know what can and can't be achieved. Data science is useful and it can be a very powerful tool for an organization, but it's not all purpose and all knowing. And so, there are often problems that just can't be solved with data science. That could be because the data aren't available. It could be because algorithms aren't good enough to be able to do that kind of prediction at that time. It could be because we can definitely solve the problem, but we just can't scale it up to the scale that's necessary. Manageres need to kind of have an idea of what are the global parameters of what can be done and what can't be done with data science. Strong communication skills are important for a manager because they are going to be communicating with their own team and interfacing with other units. Manageres need to be able to communicate with what's going on.

What is the background of data managers? Data managers ideally come from some sort of data science background. Whether that's analyzing data themselves, or building data science infrastructure themselves, plus some management training. Another option is that you have some management experience, but you've also taken or learned a little bit about data science and data engineering. And ideally you've learned about it at least at the depth where you'll be able to come up with those suggestions if the people doing the work get stuck. At the high level it's good that you know how to direct and set priorities, and know what's possible and not possible, but ideally you can also sort of get in the mix and help people out if that's possible. The best managers at some level or another know enough data science or data in general that they can contribute to the team in that way.

Their key characteristics are that they're knowledgeable about data science and they're supportive. Data science and data engineering are often very frustrating components of being in an organization for lots of different reasons. And so, being positive and supportive and motivational is really important when identifying a data science manager. Being thick-skinned is also really important, it often falls on the data science manager to report disappointing results from a prediction algorithm, or an experiment that failed, and they often have to report that to management or people that might not be too happy about it. And so, they have to be willing to do that in a way that's positive and friendly and quickly moves on to the next thing.

Data science managers advocate for and use data science in a way that's really positive for the whole organization and for their team. You're looking for somebody that can organize the whole process, keep it going, and move people onto the right problems and solve the real problems that your organization has.

Assembling the Team

Where to Find the Data Team

Now that you know the qualifications of data scientists, data engineers, and data science managers, you need to know where you can go and find those sorts of people. The obvious place to look is the general purpose sites, LinkedIn or Monster.com or something like that, where you go out and you search for data science. This can be a little bit hard to do, because there are a large number of people that call themselves data scientists. It's a hot area right now and it can be a little bit hard to identify who are the people that are really good from who are the people that aren't necessarily good. Now it's not impossible, you can look for the right programming languages for each of the different roles. You can look for past experience. Ideally they have some kind of projects online, whether that's through something like a GitHub profile where they show their software or hardware background. So ideally you have some sort of toehold on what they know if you go to these sort of general purpose sites.

Another place that you can go is you can go to is more dedicated sites. The site kaggle.com hosts data science competitions and also has a very large job board with lots of people who are looking for data science jobs. There you'll find people who have at least a little bit of experience in data science, because you also know if they've competed in competitions, what their skills are, and how they're doing. You can go to places like Insight Data Science, or you can go to places like hire.com. These are more dedicated places that are focused exclusively on hiring and building data scientists so you know a little bit more about their qualifications. There's less of a filtering process which may or may not be useful, depending on how specific are the needs of your institution or your organization versus what's being trained or what they list in these particular websites. If you're looking for somebody that's a little outside the mold, maybe the general purpose site might be better with a little bit more searching. If you're looking for sort of a more traditional data scientist or data engineer, you might go to these more specific sites.

You can also look at people's profiles on GitHub or other sites where they put up all their data science projects. This way you can get a little bit of a feel for how they work right from the start, before you even interview them. So you can go search for them through the sort of sites where they might have information posted because most of the online programs programs have them build portfolios or profiles which they put online, which makes it easier for you to find them.

Interviewing for Data Science

So once you've identified the people that you want to bring in, or people who've applied to your organization, the next step is interviewing them, and trying to figure out if they're a good fit for your data science team. The structure of a data science interview is usually is follows. Usually you meet either one on one with the candidate or you have a small group of people meet with them. Then you have some kind of demonstration or presentation, and then a demonstration of their technical skills. Those are usually the three main components of the data science interview so we will discuss each of these.

First is individual meetings or group meetings. How many people they'll meet at once, whether it's a few people, or one person, kind of depends on the size of your organization. Ideally they will meet both people inside the data science team as well as people outside the data science team, so you can get feedback on whether they've communicated well with both internal people and external people. So the key here is to focus on the projects that they've worked on. Try to illicit as much information as you can about how they work on projects. Whether they're go-getters, whether they can go figure it out on their own. The resume will tell you a lot about their technical skills but it will tell very little about their interpersonal skills. So this is a critical stage where you need to dissect and identify whether they are a person that will easily work with other people in your organisation.

Ideally, you want to do this in such a way that you include people can make people a little uncomfortable as data scientists. That's going to be part of their job is they might come up with ideas or come to conclusions that aren't super popular. But you might still want to be able to communicate with them, and you'll be able to do that in a friendly way. Here you're going to want to focus on the global evaluation of skills. Some people have used technical recruiting questions. Although, a lot of large organizations, including really famous data science organizations, have kind of moved away from that in interviews (i.e. the riddle type of questions, or the mathematical type puzzle questions are sort of not in favor any more). The reason is that it's not very useful to know how somebody is going to react to a specific tricky puzzle in a very confined setting. It's better to ask general purpose questions. How would you tackle this kind of problem? How would you, in general, build out the infrastructure to solve this kind of security risk? You want to focus on their conceptual understanding. Do they know how to tackle the problems? Do they know the right sort of language to speak? Do they know the right technologies to talk about? Do they seem like they have experience in solving the sorts of problems that you'd ask them to solve if they came onto your organization?

The next key component, and some organizations don't do this, but I think it's very important when interviewing any data scientist, data engineer, or data science manager, is to have them do some kind of demonstration or presentation. This is good for a couple of reasons. One, it's an ability for them to show their own creativity and show their own unique contribution that they can bring to your organization. If they do a presentation about a data analysis they've done, or an infrastructure they've built, or they demo some software that they build, or if they talk a little bit about their management techniques and how they would manage a data science team, it's important to get information about what's creative or unique about them.

The demonstration or presentation is also a communications skills check. Almost always data scientist, data engineers, data managers, are going to have to present their results to people. And so, it's good to evaluate right from the get-go, are they able to do that, are they able to answer questions on their feet. Are they comfortable with presenting information that's technical and detailed. It's also an opportunity for a broader group to interact with them. So you can only have so many individual or small group meetings with any person at any given day. But if you have a nice big presentation for them to give with a larger group of people, it gives more people a chance to sort of weigh in on. Does this person seem like the kind of person that would fit into our organization?

Finally, there's often an evaluation of technical skills. Now, there are two kind of schools of thought here. One is very technical, maybe even using riddle-like problems. The other is to actually have them try to solve a very small but real problem. So I think that the latter case is usually much more effective. For a data scientist, you might give them a very small data set, and see if they can do an analysis on it and report the results. It might take them only an hour because it's very small, or perhaps overnight if it's a somewhat larger problem. Afterwards you have an interview with them, go through what they did, and get a feel for what their thinking process is really like. Ideally, you'd give them a problem or a project that's related to what your organization does every day. It might be a simulated example or a fake example, so they don't get access to any real data, but it gives you an idea. How are they going to operate day-to-day in the organization?

Those are the three components, you have individual or group meetings. You have a demonstration or presentation, and then you have some evaluation of their technical skills. Then you collect all the information from everybody who saw them, and you make a judgment on whether they're a right fit for your organization.

Management Strategies

Onboarding the Data Science Team

Once you've hired a member of the data science team and they show up on their first day of work, it's important that you have a system in place so that they can quickly get into the flow. It's really easy to waste a lot of time if you don't have a system for them to get all of the support and the help that they need to get up and running as quickly as possible and really start helping your organization as fast as they can. The onboarding process for a new person usually starts with an initial meeting with whoever their manager is. As a manager, you should

- Go through an overview of their position and what the expectations are. In particular, what are the projects that you'd like to have them complete.
- Let them know who they are supposed to interact with and at what time scale.
- Let them know whether you going to initiate interactions with others, or whether they need to go and start those interactions themselves.
- Give them the contact information of any of the people that they need to be in contact with throughout the entire process.

Often, it makes a lot of sense to set up policies for how you're going to interact with the internal team. How are you going to communicate with them? What's okay and what's not okay in terms of feedback and review? The same sort of thing for external interactions. How are you going to interact with other people? Is that all going to flow through the management of the data science team? Or is that going to be embedding people briefly in other teams during the week? And how are they going to communicate with them? All of that needs to be laid out, ideally in a short, initial meeting where they actually get all that information in a compressed form. It's really ideal if that information could be stored somewhere internally on a level that they can interact with. Whether it's a website, or some kind of document that's distributed, so that they can always have a reference for who they should be contacting, how they should be acting, and so forth. So, that's the ideal way to make sure that they always have that information available to them.

The next step is usually human resources. They need to get set up with payroll, benefits, and obtain any kind of documentation they need. This isn't really part of the data science process, but it is always a step that needs to happen in the onboarding process for people.

The next thing that needs to happen is introductions. This new person might have interviewed, and others might even be aware that they're showing up, but it's really good to have that person be able to go around and put a face to the name for all the people within the data science team. It's ideal if you, as the manager, can go and take them from place to place, introduce them to all the data science team, make sure they get to know them, give them a few minutes to talk, so everybody knows who the new member of the team is. You also might want to introduce them their external points of contact. Whatever external units they'll be working with, or collaborators they'll be working with, make sure that you do a direct introduction of them, so that everyone knows the new person is here. If you initiate that yourself, then it makes it a little bit smoother for them to know where to go in the organization.

Another thing that all data scientists or data engineers will need is equipment and communications. So often they'll either have a computer, or you'll need to get them a computer associated with the activity of what they're going to be doing. Let them know what software is available for them to install, what their purchasing limits are in terms of organizing how they can get software. You also need to let them know how to interact with your global infrastructure. How do they do data pulls? What's their username? How do they interact with the infrastructure and the hardware that you have? Ideally, you have documentation for this, whether it's a PDF or some other documentation that you can give them through the internal communication channels, that shows them where all the data is stored, what kind of database you're using, and the way to pull data out of that database. Essentially, this could be tutorials and introductions, so they can immediately get up and running without having to go and ask a hundred questions of the data engineer.

Get new people quickly set up on the communication channels that are useful for you. Some organizations like to just communicate by email or through chat, with something like Slack, where they communicate with each other as a team. It's important that you get them set up and running on whatever the communication channel is, the one that your organization particularly focuses on.

After you've got their equipment set up and you've got them sort of ready to go, the best thing to do with any data scientist or data engineer is to set them up with an initial problem. Obviously what you'd like is that this person can come in and immediately start having an impact, and immediately identify all of the problems your organization might need to have solved, but that usually never happens. Each organization is a little bit quirky. They have particular problems that they care about and that they don't care about. And so the best way to get somebody up and running immediately, is to start them on small, finite, concrete project right away. This might be, for a data scientist, an analysis that is just a small analysis, that they can work on right away, that day. They can already start asking questions, and they can already start interacting with people.

It's the same story for data engineers or data science managers. You want to give them a short, concrete project that they can use as a jump start. Eventually, you're going to want them to work on larger scale projects. But if they get something under their belt, right away, that's a solution they can present, first of all, and it gives them confidence. Second of all, the best way to get them integrated into a team is to have them working on a project right away.

So, the first thing that you do, is you give them that initial project, along with all of the other documentation that you need, and then, you turn them loose.

Managing the Team

Once your team is up and running, the process of managing or maintaining the team as it goes forward and answers data science problems is a critical role for a data science manager. The first thing that you would often have with every member of your team, ideally, is individual meetings. This will happen if you are at the first stage of management where you're managing just a few people. Once your organization gets a little bit bigger, there'll be a hierarchical structure and you might not necessarily meet with every member of the team every week say. But if you're only managing a few people, it's a really good idea to have a standing regular meeting where they can come and they can present anything that they're working on, things that they've accomplished, or things that they finished and so you can sort of check them off as things that have gotten done. They can also discuss any kind of problems that they have and their goals for the week. Individual meetings take up a lot of time, but they can be a huge advantage in the sense that people often get stuck in data science on something that can easily be resolved just by having someone else look at it. This is the best and most effective way to get people unstuck and keep them moving.

The second thing that makes a lot of sense to have is Data Science Team Meetings. So that's get the whole data science team together. Again, this should be a regular standing meeting that you have so that everybody can come together and talk about what they're working on. They can share any updates of any progress that they've made. They can identify any problems that they are working on, or that they're stuck on, particularly problems that maybe touch on different teams. For example, suppose the data science team can't necessarily make a data pull that they want because the infrastructure isn't in place. That's a good time to communicate with the data engineering team. And then what are their goals? What are the steps that they want to take? It's also an opportunity to peer review the progress that's being made. Data science teams can make presentations or data engineering teams can make presentations. Everyone else can chip in, and make comments and evaluate.

The key here is that you need to set it up in such a way, that people are empowered or able to make criticism if they need to. They can make critical comments about other people's stuff without being rude or mean. There's a very fine line to balance, and a lot of people have difficulty with giving criticism well or taking criticism well. It's up to the data science team lead to make sure that, especially when dealing with data, to be very objective to allow people to express their real opinions. It's also an opportunity for you to set team priorities and motivate people. Data science can very often become a slog and it's very hard to get all the details right when you're doing an analysis or setting up an infrastructure. When you're mired in the weeds, it's very helpful to have somebody who can come in and tell you the bigger picture. Why are we doing this? Why are we solving all these really hard technical problems? What's the goal that we're setting and how do we get there? That's your opportunity to motivate people, keep everybody excited, and keep everybody fresh on the problems that you're working on at any given time. It's important to have both individual meetings, where each person can talk about what are their personal issues that they need to deal with or their own personal successes, and also a group meeting where everybody can come together and communicate.

You're also in charge of monitoring interactions. It's very common, if you set your data science team up in the way that is the most optimal, to have a data science team that sits all by itself, that talks to each other and so forth. But then those people also in the data science team spend some period of time embedded in other groups. They email those other groups, and ideally each member of your team will be responsible for interacting with one particular external unit of the organization that you're dealing with. So it's your job to keep on top of that. To monitor how those interactions are going you can either do that actively, by being CC'd on messages, by being involved in the Slack channel or by going to those meetings with the external folks. Or you can do it sort of more passively, sort of accept the feedback and hear it from both the external organization and from the person that you've embedded there. In either case, it's up to you to monitor that and make sure that the communication is flowing.

A very common occurrence is either for communication to be too fast or too slow, in a sense that if it's too slow, the're not getting enough details back and forth, and the progress will slow down. If it's to fast, you might have an external unit that's making extreme demands on the data scientist. That's very common too, and so knowing how to modulate those sorts of requests and take some of the heat for the data scientist or data engineer that's getting those requests is something that is up to the data manager. It's up to you to keep things running, and so the best way to do this in my experience is with an open door policy. Generally it's good to have people be able to come to you at anytime and not just at their weekly meeting or their regular individual meeting or group meeting. Have them be able to just drop by and ask questions so that they can immediately get unstuck. Some of these details are things where people get stuck for a long time on something that can easily be solved if they talked to somebody else. And so the best way to do that is Is to have an open policy. Another way is to have a policy to quickly respond to questions via email or chat, especially if they're things that can be resolved very quickly. You also want to be able to minimize the amount of formal meetings that people have. There needs to be a regular meeting so you can check on progress but you don't want to introduce a large number of meetings. Data science and data engineering require large amounts of uninterrupted, concentrated effort, and so introducing too many meetings into the lives of these people means that they'll really slow down their work. One way to do that is by allowing quick communication that doesn't have to resolve into a formalized meeting.

It's also important to manage the growth of the organization and that's growth in a couple of different ways. Obviously it's growth in terms of the number of people and how they're going to be managed and how they can communicate with each other and so forth. But it's also good to manage the growth of individual people. Make sure that there are opportunities for them to learn new tools. Whether that's through giving them access to courses online or otherwise. Whether it's through presentations in the group meeting, where people present new ideas or new tools that they've learned about so other people can take advantage of them. Whether its introductions to new interactions. So sometimes you'll be in meetings that aren't necessarily the meetings that your data science team is going to, but you might identify an external group or a person that really would make a good connection with your data science team. It's your job as the data science manager to facilitate that interaction.

A really critical component of being a data science manager is, and building a good data science team, is identifying opportunities for advancement for your people. Anytime that there's an opportunity for your people to either get promoted or to take on new responsibilities that will look really good for them on their resume, it's up to the data science manager to sort of be on the lookout for those opportunities. This can happen through new interactions, through learning about new tools, or through ways in which they can promote themselves both inside the organization and externally at conferences or at meet-ups, or anything like that where they can actually make more connections in their field.

Working With Other Teams

Embedded vs. Dedicated

One of the questions that often comes up when building a data science team, is whether you should build a stand-alone data science group all on it's own, or whether you should embed data scientists, one in each of a number of different external management organizations. In the embedded data scientist idea, you're taking a data scientist and you're having them sit with say, the marketing team, or you're having them sit with the business intelligence team, or you're having them sit with a different team than the rest of their data science colleagues. There are some big advantages to this approach. In particular, the data scientist gets to hear about the problems every day that that organization is having and it's a really great way to promote collaboration. It's also a little bit difficult because the data scientists can't necessarily communicate very well with their own or other data scientists. They won't be able to ask questions if they get stuck on different problems.

On the other hand, you could imagine setting up a independent data science group. So this depends a little bit on the scale of your organization. If you're a really small start-up organization with only one or two people, there's no need for a dedicated group. But for a larger organization, sometimes it makes sense to have them all sit together. The advantage here is that they'll be able to ask questions quickly of their peers, they'll have good support among them. The disadvantage is that they won't necessarily be on top of all the problems that necessarily they need to be on top of in order to do their job and to effectively use data for your organization. The key points when making this comparison are *communication, support,* and *empowerment* of data scientists.

- **Communication**. A data scientist needs to be working on a concrete problem and those concrete problems often don't come out of the data science team. They often come out of another team, whether that's the marketing team, or whether that's the leadership, or some other part of the company or organization that you are working for. To have close communication, one option is to embed the person directly in that external unit and have them talk to them all the time. But another way is to make sure that the channels of communication are open between people in the external units and people in the data science team. Either way, the key component is that the data scientist should always be aware of what's the concrete problem they're trying to solve? And when they come up with solutions, they need to know what to benchmark against, to know what does success look like? The best way to do that is through communication with these external units.
- **Support**. You need to support data scientists, and not only support data scientists, but that way they have the support they need to be able to help the other people in your organization. If a data scientist is embedded in an external unit, often they don't necessarily have another person that they can talk to. It can be very frustrating to perform data science. A lot of the job is very low-level data cleaning, which can be a very painful. The idea is you want to be able to have somebody that they can turn to, that they can talk to for

advice or support. That often is more available in a stand-alone data science unit. They can actually go and talk to other people. But again, this can lead to an insular nature of the group being on its own.

- **Empowerment**. One thing that's very difficult about being a data scientist in an organization is that the data often don't tell you what you want to hear. So it's very common to run an experiment and to get a result that goes against the common wisdom. Or maybe you have a great idea, a great hypothesis, so you run an experiment, and you collect the data and it turns out your hypothesis was wrong. Communicating these sorts of things to the people that had the ideas or the external units that came up with those projects can be very difficult. In particular, if the external units are upset about the results that came out of the data science project, there can be a problem because the data scientists might be incentivized to not tell you the full truth, or to not communicate exactly what happened in the experiment. Thereforew you need to empower data scientists to be able to be confident in reporting the results that were there and then to have the organization support that and make quick decisions, even when those decisions are not necessarily the way that everyone would want to work. Doing data science is not a political process, which can often make the politics very difficult for data scientists.

One happy medium between the two ways of working, whether you embed somebody out externally, or you have a dedicated team, is to, once you're at a scale that's useful for it, have the team sit together in a way that they can all communicate with each other. They can commiserate with each other, they can empower each other to feel good about the decisions they're making about what to report.

But then you make sure that they have close contact and continual contact with external groups. They might go sit for an hour a week with some group or they might go sit for a couple hours a week with another group. But they always have a home base to come back to, the data science home base, where they can feel really supported and they can have the right people to ask questions about. As long as you can encourage the right kind of communication and make sure that the team doesn't become insular, that usually tends to be the optimal arrangement, a dedicated team with close connections to individual groups. Ideally, each person on the team has one external unit that they are responsible for, or a small number of units that they're responsible for, so that they can develop long-term relationships with those units and really be effective at using data to help optimize the organization.

How Does Data Science Interact with Other Groups?

Once you have a data science team, you need to think about how that team is going to interact with other teams within your organization. There a few different modes under which that can happen.

- **Consulting**. Consulting is an opportunity for your team to collaborate with other people where they come to you. They bring problems from outside that they want to have solved, whether it's predicting how many people will come to a certain website, or identifying how many people will click on an ad. Or any other kind of problem that's based in something that they're working on that they think machine learning, or prediction, or inference would help them out with. So that's a consulting model where they sort of come to you.

- **Collaboration**. In collaboration, the data science team will work closely with one of your external teams to sort of build out a whole project. In that case, it might be long-term, in the sense that you might have one data scientist working with an external team, (e.g. the marketing team) for a long period of time, or with one collaborator for a long period of time. In that case, you often build a sort of a deeper knowledge of the exact role of that external person, and so that can often help in the data science process. When you're talking about just a consulting relationship, you only get a superficial idea about what the problem is that you're solving. Data science can still be useful, but it really doesn't have that deep dive effect where the person actually has expertise in the area that they're working on.

- **Teaching**. Almost all data science organizations can play a useful role by educating other people about what data science is and what data science can be used for. This is one way that the team can actually help benefit all the different teams within the organization or the other collaborative groups within the organization. A teaching role for a data science unit is always a very helpful component. One way to do that is to organize one-off events where you have a particular idea that's taught, say, how to visualize data or how to interact with data. Another is to have a standing teaching commitment where you have a boot camp for people that come in.

Finally, you can have a data science team be creative and propose new ideas and actually move the organization forward. There's an idea that you could be data-driven, in a sense that you can go out and collect data, and make all of your decisions based on the data wisdom that you collect from those experiments. But that actually falls a little short of being able really make transformative changes based on data. In order to make transformative changes with data, you need to propose new hypotheses and then test those hypotheses and see if they actually work. So it might be creating a new product and then running experiments to see if that product works. Or might be predicting consumer behavior or any kind of behavior that you're interested in, based on machine learning, in a new way, in a new application. Those sorts of creative ideas can often come from the data science team, particularly if they're involved in those sort of close collaborative relationships where they really understand what's the problem we're trying to solve. Maybe they have a new idea or some new data that they can go collect, either within your organization or externally, to answer that question. So it's always great to give your data science team a little bit of freedom to be creative and to come up with their own ideas.

Empowering Others to Use Data

It's not just the people in your data dcience team that will want to use and interact with data. So part of your role as data science manager, or as a data science executive is teaching people how to use data or empowering people to use data within an organization. One of the ways in which to do that is through data science training. There are a number of different ways that you can do this. One is pointing people to resources, collecting and curating resources that are available online. Whether that's online classes or online materials related to sorts of things that they might want to be able to do. It might be writing those tutorials yourself, so that people can interact with the data themselves directly.

Another really useful way is to have internal talks that are available to everybody to go to if they want to where the data dcience team communicates how do you pull data out of the database? How do you make plots? How do you visualize data in a way that's compelling? How do you do machine learning? Or what is machine learning? Those internal talks are really useful if they can also communicate what the internal capabilities are. One thing that's very difficult about data science teams is that every sata science team has different capabilities. Depending on the people that are there, how subscribed their activities are, and how difficult it is to do the problems. Communicating what's possible and what's not possible in a way that's unbiased to the whole organization often spurs new ideas. New ways to take advantage of the data science team to solve new problems that people care about. You can either have training sessions or informational sessions about how the data science team works. Those are both really useful ways to empower people to approach the data science team and work with them.

Another way is to build documents or build tools or build products that can be shared with other people who don't necessarily have data science or data engineering training, but would like to interact with the data. One common example is a dashboard, a set of visualizations or set of plots that are built so that somebody can click on some buttons and interact with that visualization. They can ask their own questions, have their own hypothesis and interact with the data, even if it's just a subset of the data. Another way is just one interactive visualization can be really compelling, that can be a way for people to interact with the data, ask one specific question, and see how their choices work. Here the key is, there's a design element to it—how are you going to design your interface so that people can interact with the data? They can ask their own questions but they're not intimidated by syntax or knowing how to actually do the stuff with the low-level programming languages that you or your data science team might know about. In addition to training, there's these ways to directly connect people to the data themselves. Ideally, you can automate this. So a lot of report writing tools, whether they're in iPython notebooks or shiny documents or so forth, can be auto-generated. You can also setup a dashboard that does an auto-pull from your database, that always has the latest and freshest data available to people. If you can automate it in that way, the most common questions can be answered by people other than the data science team which leads them to innovate and to focus on new ideas and new things that they can do well

The other thing that can be really useful as a way to have people interact with the data science team is with data science idea evaluation. So often people will have ideas about ways they think they might be able to use data that solve a particular problem or another. But it turns out that sometimes those are impossible. We don't have the right data or we don't have the imaginary infrastructure, we don't have the right scale to be able to solve that problem. But it's still really nice if you can provide a way or a format or a forum where people can propose ideas that they'd like to do with the data and get critical, but positive feedback on those ideas. You don't want to immediately crush any idea that somebody brings up. You'll never hear another idea again. But it is a good idea that helps tune expectations. What can we actually do with the datasets that we have? Especially, if someone else is proposing the ideas and you are letting them know, for example,

- Yes, we can do that

- No, we can't do that
- Yes, we can do that, but it would take a whole new infrastructure on the server side.
- Yes, we can do that, but it would require us to develop a whole new machine learning infrastructure here.

That gives people an idea about what's going on with the data science team, what can you actually do, what are the parameters that makes it useful for you. You can do peer review of these ideas from the data team and from yourself as another way to interact with the organization. But in general, the idea is as often as possible drawing other people into the data science process. Often that requires a little bit of education and that education can feel like wasted time if you're not thinking about it in the right way. But if you think about it as an investment in the future data science capabilities of your organization. It can be a really positive, really value compounding way of doing data science.

Common Difficulties

Interaction Difficulties

No matter how well you've put the data science team together, there can often be problems when the data science team is interacting with people outside of the team but within your organization. This section talks a little bit about what those problems are and how to deal with them.

The first one is lack of interaction. This can happen especially if you have a data science team that's stand alone and there's not necessarily a standing commitment, to be embedded with or sitting with an external unit. If there's a lack of interaction, you have to identify what the problem is. The problem can either be with the data scientists—they don't know how to contact the person or they don't know what questions to be asking—or it could be with the external unit. Sometimes that lack of communication is because there is nothing to do. So you need to identify if this is because there's not actually a problem for them to be solving. In this case it's good to repurpose that data scientist's time on to a different project. It might be because the external person isn't necessarily contacting the data scientists or because your data scientist is so busy working on a problem that they're not interacting—they're not emailing and contacting the person that they're working with. This will depend a little bit on the scale of the project. If you're building a quick machine learning algorithm, there should be lots of quick interaction. If you're building out a huge scalable infrastructure for data management, it might take a little bit longer before there's interaction with the leadership team about that, and that's to be expected.

If there's a lack of communication, there are a few options. You can take a more active role: Start initiating the conversation or send emails that will connect people together. You have to be very mindful of the balance of not interrupting time for data scientists and data engineers. Those sorts of uninterrupted moments are when most of the work gets done. If you need to move personnel from a project, whether it's for lack of motivation, lack of good communication, or because there's not really a data science project they're going to be working on, that's an important part of a data science manager, or an executive's job.

Another reason that you might have to get involved is lack of empowerment. This often happens if the data scientist is actually embedded in an external team. If this is the situation, often the data scientist will feel a little bit isolated and they might not feel empowered to make decisions. The external unit is in charge. They have to make some decisions about marketing or they have to make some decisions about how they're going to take that data and make a decision for a product and so forth. Because data scientists in this situation don't necessarily make those decisions, they might feel that they keep presenting data ideas and showing them experimental results and they just don't listen.

The first thing that you need to do is understand both sides, because problems can arise in one of two ways in this situation. One, the external person that they're working with can just be ignoring their advice, ignoring their data analysis. In that case, it's up to you to convince the external person, and to take the initiative to explain why this is important, why using the data will help you do a better job, will get you better results at the end of the day. On the other hand, it could be because the data scientist is just pushing ideas beyond the scope of the data, or they're not getting the data analysis done in a way that's convincing for the external person to look at and interact with.

One thing that's a common misconception about data science or data engineering is that it's basically instantaneous. Because computers are so fast, people think that also data science or machine learning is really fast to develop. But sometimes it isn't. Sometimes it takes a long time to build a really good machine learning algorithm. Part of your role is being the intermediate. Being the explainer. Why does it take so long? And then providing internal support to your data science team. And whether that's just being an ear for them to talk to or by suggesting new ideas. Very often it's by identifying when to stop. Data science and data engineering are often areas where perfect is the enemy of the very good. Once you have a pretty good solution, that might be enough to get everything done. The data scientists or data engineers, because they have pride in what they're doing, may try to optimize that machine learning algorithm for the last 3% accuracy, or save a little bit more computing power on the data engineering side. Sometimes that's necessary, but sometimes it isn't, and it's up to the data science manager to pay attention and manage when you're actually solving the data science problem that matters versus when you're chasing something that doesn't maybe necessarily matter in the grand scheme of things.

The last problem can be lack of understanding. This could be because the data science team doesn't understand the problem that they're working on. This commonly happens when a data scientist acts in a consulting roll, when they just do a one off. People from your organization might bring one question, asking "How does this t-test work?" or "How does this random forest work?" In that case, the data scientist might not actually understand the underlying problem, and so they might give advice that isn't very good. Another way that this could work is, the marketing team doesn't understand what data science can do, or the product team doesn't understand what data science can do, or any collaborator doesn't understand what data science can do. It's up to you to help make sure that everyone knows what's possible and what's not possible.

You can manage this process in a few different ways. First, make sure that, if you have a separate dedicated data science team, that they interact with other groups in a regular way, that they're embedded for periods of time. You can ensure that there's presentations regularly to the organization both about capabilities and about new techniques and about just what's going on. Advertising the data science team within the organization can ensure that everyone knows that certain kinds of problems are problems that the data science team can handle. These are the sorts of things that can help build a understanding within the organization about what data science is and how it can help. These are a few of the ways that you could help minimize external conflicts within the data science team.

Internal Difficulties

No matter how well you set up your data science team, and no matter how nice the personalities are, there will always be some internal difficulties. Some of these are related to personalities and interactions between people. Some of them are related to the way data scientists and data engineers tend to work. It's up to you to set up an environment where these sorts of problems are minimized and it's possible to keep the process moving as quickly and as friendly a way as possible.

The first thing that can happen is there can be interpersonal conflict. This happens in any organization, but when you're dealing with heavily quantitative folks who often are a little bit introverted and maybe have a little bit less interpersonal interaction than people in other external units might have, you can end up with some difficulties of interaction. It's very helpful to right up front have a policy on the Code of Conduct. This policy can cover all sorts of things, but it should definitely cover all of the biggies. Obviously, you don't want to have any put downs on the basis of sexual orientation or on the basis of race or on the basis of sex. All of that can be built into the policy, but it can also cover more subtle things and data science specific things.

For example, if there's going to be code review, if one person is going to review someone else's code, you might set up the parameters for how that's going to happen. Are they going to make the suggestions? Are they going to immediately submit changes or fixes to people's code? Are they going to do that in a way where they communicate with the person who originally wrote the code or not? When people are reviewing each other's code and in group meeting how are they supposed to communicate? Are they supposed to be critical? How are they supposed to be impartial? How are they supposed to interact with each other? Now this seems a little bit pedantic to have these sorts of things set up in advance, but it can really save you a lot of trouble in the long run. It also helps becuse in a data science organization there are often uncomfortable truths that you discover with data. Whether it's something you didn't quite expect or a product or a machine learning algorithm that failed. Having a Code of Contact in place to prevent personal feelings from being hurt is a critical component.

In that Code of Conduct it also makes a lot of sense to explain what you mean by success and failure. If you only

define success by the machine learning algorithm works or
the software never has bugs in it or the hardware never
goes down, there will be a lot of failure. But if you define
success as identifying problems, tackling those problems,
and not always getting an answer that everyone expects,
you reduce the pressure on any individual analysis, and that
allows people to act more impartially and really let the data
speak for itself.

In addition to this policy you need to have open communication. Allow people to communicate directly with you,
and with each other, about whether that policy is being
enforced. And make sure that they feel empowered to have
that conversation with each other. This is critically important, both in a general sense, but also very specifically for
data science. It needs to be a policy that open criticism
of each others' data analysis, or other people's data infrastructure, is accepted and embraced, but at the same time,
isn't made to make people feel awful or isn't used to hurt
people. It's just used to improve the entire process. If you
organize it in that way, people will be open to criticism and
they'll be willing to make changes if they don't feel like it's
going to hurt their job and their job prospects. The other
thing is, in the extreme circumstance where people are not
adhering to the Code of Conduct, for either general purpose
reasons or for data science specific reasons, it's very useful
to have outlined what are the steps that are going to take
place. What's the enforcement? Whether it's something like,
"I'm going to point out when you're behaving incorrectly in
a code review" or whether it's something like at a certain
stage, you'll be barred from coming to this meeting for this
period of time. Whatever it is that you need to establish,
it's better to say it up front, rather than to invent policies
on the fly when dealing with a data science team, especially
when you're dealing with diverse people who have different

expertise, and maybe different expectations about what's going on.

Managing Data Analysis

Note: Much of the material in this chapter is expanded upon in the book *The Art of Data Science* by Peng and Matsui, which is available from Leanpub.

The Data Analysis Iteration

Watch a video: Data Analysis Iteration | Stages of Data Analysis

To the uninitiated, a data analysis may appear to follow a linear, one-step-after-the-other process which at the end, arrives at a nicely packaged and coherent result. In reality, data analysis is a highly iterative and non-linear process, better reflected by a series of epicycles (see Figure), in which information is learned at each step, which then informs whether (and how) to refine, and redo, the step that was just performed, or whether (and how) to proceed to the next step.

An epicycle is a small circle whose center moves around the circumference of a larger circle. In data analysis, the iterative process that is applied to all steps of the data analysis can be conceived of as an epicycle that is repeated for each step along the circumference of the entire data analysis process. Some data analyses appear to be fixed and linear, such as algorithms embedded into various software platforms, including apps. However, these algorithms are final data analysis products that have emerged from the very non-linear work of developing and refining a data analysis so that it can be algorithmized.

Epicycle of Analysis

There are 5 core activities of data analysis:

1. Stating and refining the question

2. Exploring the data
3. Building formal statistical models
4. Interpreting the results
5. Communicating the results

These 5 activities can occur at different time scales: for example, you might go through all 5 in the course of a day, but also deal with each, for a large project, over the course of many months. Before discussing these core activities, which will occur in later chapters, it will be important to first understand the overall framework used to approach each of these activities.

Although there are many different types of activities that you might engage in while doing data analysis, every aspect of the entire process can be approached through an interative process that we call the *epicycle of data analysis*. More specifically, for each of the five core activities, it is critical that you engage in the following steps:

1. Setting Expectations,
2. Collecting information (data), comparing the data to your expectations, and if the expectations don't match,
3. Revising your expectations or fixing the data so your data and your expectations match.

As you go through every stage of an analysis, you will need to go through the epicycle to continuously refine your question, your exploratory data analysis, your formal models, your interpretation, and your communication.

The repeated cycling through each of these five core activities that is done to complete a data analysis forms the larger circle of data analysis. In this chapter we go into detail about what this 3-step epicyclic process is and give examples of how you can apply it to your data analysis.

Developing expectations is the process of deliberately thinking about what you expect before you do anything, such as inspect your data, perform a procedure, or enter a command. For experienced data analysts, in some circumstances, developing expectations may be an automatic, almost subconscious process, but it's an important activity to cultivate and be deliberate about.

For example, you may be going out to dinner with friends at a cash-only establishment and need to stop by the ATM to withdraw money before meeting up. To make a decision about the amount of money you're going to withdraw, you have to have developed some expectation of the cost of dinner. This may be an automatic expectation because you dine at this establishment regularly so you know what the typical cost of a meal is there, which would be an example of *a priori* knowledge. Another example of *a priori* knowledge would be knowing what a typical meal costs at a restaurant in your city, or knowing what a meal at the most expensive restaurants in your city costs. Using that information, you could perhaps place an upper and lower bound on how much the meal will cost.

You may have also sought out external information to develop your expectations, which could include asking your friends who will be joining you or who have eaten at the restaurant before and/or Googling the restaurant to find general cost information online or a menu with prices. This same process, in which you use any a priori information you have and/or external sources to determine what you expect when you inspect your data or execute an analysis procedure, applies to each core activity of the data analysis process.

Collecting information entails collecting information about your question or your data. For your question, you collect information by performing a literature search or asking experts in order to ensure that your question is a good one. In the next chapter, we will discuss characteristics of a good question. For your data, after you have some expectations about what the result will be when you inspect your data or perform the analysis procedure, you then perform the operation. The results of that operation are the data you need to collect, and then you determine if the data you collected matches your expectations. To extend the restaurant metaphor, when you go to the restaurant, getting the check is collecting the data.

Now that you have data in hand (the check at the restaurant), the next step is to compare your expectations to the data. There are two possible outcomes: either your expectations of the cost matches the amount on the check, or they do not. If your expectations and the data match, terrific, you can move onto the next activity. If, on the other hand, your expectations were a cost of 30 dollars, but the check was 40 dollars, your expectations and the data do not match. There are two possible explanations for the discordance: first, your expectations were wrong and need to be revised, or second, the check was wrong and contains an error. You review the check and find that you were charged for two desserts instead of the one that you had, and conclude that there is an error in the data, so ask for the check to be corrected.

One key indicator of how well your data analysis is going is how easy or difficult it is to match the data you collected to your original expectations. You want to setup your expectations and your data so that matching the two up is easy. In the restaurant example, your expectation was $30 and the data said the meal cost $40, so it's easy to see that (a) your expectation was off by $10 and that (b) the meal was more expensive than you thought. When you come back to this place, you might bring an extra $10. If our original expectation was that the meal would be between $0 and $1,000, then it's true that our data fall into that range, but it's not clear how much more we've learned. For example, would you change your behavior the next time you came back? The expectation of a $30 meal is sometimes referred to as a sharp hypothesis because it states something very specific that can be verified with the data.

Asking the Question

Watch a video: Characteristics of a Good Question | Types of Questions

Doing data analysis requires quite a bit of thinking and we believe that when you've completed a good data analysis, you've spent more time thinking than doing. The thinking begins before you even look at a dataset, and it's well worth devoting careful thought to your question. This point cannot be over-emphasized as many of the "fatal" pitfalls of a data analysis can be avoided by expending the mental energy to get your question right. In this chapter, we will discuss the characteristics of a good question, the types of questions that can be asked, and how to apply the iterative epicyclic process to stating and refining your question so that when you start looking at data, you have a sharp, answerable question.

Types of Questions

Before we delve into stating the question, it's helpful to consider what the different types of questions are. There are six basic types of questions and much of the discussion that follows comes from a paper published in *Science* by Roger Peng and Jeff Leek. Understanding the type of question you are asking may be the most fundamental step you can take to ensure that, in the end, your interpretation of the results is correct. The six types of questions are:

1. Descriptive

2. Exploratory
3. Inferential
4. Predictive
5. Causal
6. Mechanistic

And the type of question you are asking directly informs how you interpret your results.

An *exploratory* question is one in which you analyze the data to see if there are patterns, trends, or relationships between variables. These types of analyses are also called "hypothesis-generating" analyses because rather than testing a hypothesis as would be done with an inferential, causal, or mechanistic question, you are looking for patterns that would support proposing a hypothesis. If you had a general thought that diet was linked somehow to viral illnesses, you might explore this idea by examining relationships between a range of dietary factors and viral illnesses. You find in your exploratory analysis that individuals who ate a diet high in certain foods had fewer viral illnesses than those whose diet was not enriched for these foods, so you propose the hypothesis that among adults, eating at least 5 servings a day of fresh fruit and vegetables is associated with fewer viral illnesses per year.

An *inferential* question would be a restatement of this proposed hypothesis as a question and would be answered by analyzing a different set of data, which in this example, is a representative sample of adults in the US. By analyzing this different set of data you are both determining if the association you observed in your exploratory analysis holds in a different sample and whether it holds in a sample that is representative of the adult US population, which would suggest that the association is applicable to all adults in the

US. In other words, you will be able to infer what is true, on average, for the adult population in the US from the analysis you perform on the representative sample.

A *predictive* question would be one where you ask what types of people will eat a diet high in fresh fruits and vegetables during the next year. In this type of question you are less interested in what causes someone to eat a certain diet, just what predicts whether someone will eat this certain diet. For example, higher income may be one of the final set of predictors, and you may not know (or even care) why people with higher incomes are more likely to eat a diet high in fresh fruits and vegetables, but what is most important is that income is a factor that predicts this behavior.

Although an inferential question might tell us that people who eat a certain type of foods tend to have fewer viral illnesses, the answer to this question does not tell us if eating these foods causes a reduction in the number of viral illnesses, which would be the case for a *causal* question. A causal question asks about whether changing one factor will change another factor, on average, in a population. Sometimes the underlying design of the data collection, by default, allows for the question that you ask to be causal. An example of this would be data collected in the context of a randomized trial, in which people were randomly assigned to eat a diet high in fresh fruits and vegetables or one that was low in fresh fruits and vegetables. In other instances, even if your data are not from a randomized trial, you can take an analytic approach designed to answer a causal question.

Finally, none of the questions described so far will lead to an answer that will tell us, if the diet does, indeed, cause a reduction in the number of viral illnesses, *how* the diet leads to a reduction in the number of viral illnesses. A question that asks how a diet high in fresh fruits and vegetables leads to a reduction in the number of viral illnesses would be a *mechanistic* question.

There are a couple of additional points about the types of questions that are important. First, by necessity, many data analyses answer multiple types of questions. For example, if a data analysis aims to answer an inferential question, descriptive and exploratory questions must also be answered during the process of answering the inferential question. To continue our example of diet and viral illnesses, you would not jump straight to a statistical model of the relationship between a diet high in fresh fruits and vegetables and the number of viral illnesses without having determined the frequency of this type of diet and viral illnesses and their relationship to one another in this sample. A second point is that the type of question you ask is determined in part by the data available to you (unless you plan to conduct a study and collect the data needed to do the analysis). For example, you may want to ask a causal question about diet and viral illnesses to know whether eating a diet high in fresh fruits and vegetables causes a decrease in the number of viral illnesses, and the best type of data to answer this causal question is one in which people's diets change from one that is high in fresh fruits and vegetables to one that is not, or vice versa. If this type of data set does not exist, then the best you may be able to do is either apply causal analysis methods to observational data or instead answer an inferential question about diet and viral illnesses.

Exploratory Data Analysis

Watch a video: EDA Part 1 | EDA Part 2 | EDA Part 3 | EDA Part 4

Exploratory data analysis is the process of exploring your data, and it typically includes examining the structure and components of your dataset, the distributions of individual variables, and the relationships between two or more variables. The most heavily relied upon tool for exploratory data analysis is visualizing data using a graphical representation of the data. Data visualization is arguably the most important tool for exploratory data analysis because the information conveyed by graphical display can be very quickly absorbed and because it is generally easy to recognize patterns in a graphical display.

There are several goals of exploratory data analysis, which are:

1. To determine if there are any problems with your dataset.
2. To determine whether the question you are asking can be answered by the data that you have.
3. To develop a sketch of the answer to your question.

Your application of exploratory data analysis will be guided by your question. The example question used in this chapter is: "Do counties in the eastern United States have higher ozone levels than counties in the western United States?" In this instance, you will explore the data to determine if there are problems with the dataset, and to determine if you can answer your question with this dataset.

To answer the question of course, you need ozone, county, and US region data. The next step is to use exploratory data analysis to begin to answer your question, which could include displaying boxplots of ozone by region of the US. At the end of exploratory data analysis, you should have a good sense of what the answer to your question is and be armed with sufficient information to move onto the next steps of data analysis.

It's important to note that here, again, the concept of the epicycle of analysis applies. You should have an expectation of what your dataset will look like and whether your question can be answered by the data you have. If the content and structure of the dataset doesn't match your expectation, then you will need to go back and figure out if your expectation was correct (but there was a problem with the data) or alternatively, your expectation was incorrect, so you cannot use the dataset to answer the question and will need to find another dataset.

You should also have some expectation of what the ozone levels will be as well as whether one region's ozone should be higher (or lower) than another's. As you move to step 3 of beginning to answer your question, you will again apply the epicycle of analysis so that if, for example, the ozone levels in the dataset are lower than what you expected from looking at previously published data, you will need to pause and figure out if there is an issue with your data or if your expectation was incorrect. Your expectation could be incorrect, for example, if your source of information for setting your expectation about ozone levels was data collected from 20 years ago (when levels were likely higher) or from only a single city in the U.S. We will go into more detail with the case study below, but this should give you an overview about the approach and goals of exploratory data analysis.

In this section we will run through an informal "checklist" of things to do when embarking on an exploratory data analysis. The elements of the checklist are

1. *Formulate your question.* We have discussed the importance of properly formulating a question. Formulating a question can be a useful way to guide the exploratory data analysis process and to limit the exponential number of paths that can be taken with any sizeable dataset. In particular, a *sharp* question or hypothesis can serve as a dimension reduction tool that can eliminate variables that are not immediately relevant to the question. It's usually a good idea to spend a few minutes to figure out what is the question you're *really* interested in, and narrow it down to be as specific as possible (without becoming uninteresting).

2. *Read in your data.* This part is obvious–without data there's no analysis. Sometimes the data will come in a very messy format and you'll need to do some cleaning. Other times, someone else will have cleaned up that data for you so you'll be spared the pain of having to do the cleaning.

3. *Check the packaging.* Assuming you don't get any warnings or errors when reading in the dataset, it's usually a good idea to poke the data a little bit before you break open the wrapping paper. For example, you should check the number of rows and columns. Often, with just a few simple maneuvers that perhaps don't qualify as real data analysis, you can nevertheless identify potential problems with the data before plunging in head first into a complicated data analysis.

4. *Look at the top and the bottom of your data.* It's often
   useful to look at the "beginning" and "end" of a dataset
   right after you check the packaging. This lets you
   know if the data were read in properly, things are
   properly formatted, and that everthing is there. If your
   data are time series data, then make sure the dates
   at the beginning and end of the dataset match what
   you expect the beginning and ending time period to
   be. Looking at the last few rows of a dataset can be
   particularly useful because often there will be some
   problem reading the end of a dataset and if you don't
   check that specifically you'd never know.

5. *Check your "n"s.* In general, counting things is usually a
   good way to figure out if anything is wrong or not. In
   the simplest case, if you're expecting there to be 1,000
   observations and it turns out there's only 20, you
   know something must have gone wrong somewhere.
   But there are other areas that you can check depending on your application. To do this properly, you need
   to identify some *landmarks* that can be used to check
   against your data. For example, if you are collecting
   data on people, such as in a survey or clinical trial, then
   you should know how many people there are in your
   study.

6. *Validate with at least one external data source.* Making sure your data matches something outside of the
   dataset is very important. It allows you to ensure that
   the measurements are roughly in line with what they
   should be and it serves as a check on what *other* things
   might be wrong in your dataset. External validation
   can often be as simple as checking your data against a
   single number.

7. *Make a plot.* Making a plot to visualize your data is
   a good way to further your understanding of your

question and your data. There are two key reasons for making a plot of your data. They are *creating expectations* and *checking deviations from expectations*. At the early stages of analysis, you may be equipped with a question/hypothesis, but you may have little sense of what is going on in the data. You may have peeked at some of it for sake of doing some sanity checks, but if your dataset is big enough, it will be difficult to simply look at all the data. Making some sort of plot, which serves as a summary, will be a useful tool for *setting expectations for what the data should look like*. Making a plot can also be a useful tool to see how well the data match your expectations. Plots are particularly good at letting you see *deviations* from what you might expect. Tables typically are good at *summarizing* data by presenting things like means, medians, or other statistics. Plots, however, can show you those things, as well as show you things that are far from the mean or median, so you can check to see if something is *supposed* to be that far away. Often, what is obvious in a plot can be hidden away in a table.

8. *Try the easy solution first.* What's the simplest answer you could provide to answer your question? For the moment, don't worry about whether the answer is 100% correct, but the point is how could you provide *prima facie* evidence for your hypothesis or question. You may refute that evidence later with deeper analysis, but this is the first pass. Importantly, if you do not find evidence of a signal in the data using just a simple plot or analysis, then often it is unlikely that you will find something using a more sophisticated analysis.

In this section we've presented some simple steps to take when starting off on an exploratory analysis. The point of this is to get you thinking about the data and the question of interest. It should also give you a number of things to follow up on in case you continue to be interested in this question. At this point it's useful to consider a few followup questions.

1. *Do you have the right data?* Sometimes at the conclusion of an exploratory data analysis, the conclusion is that the dataset is not really appropriate for this question. In that case you may need to go and get completely different data for your question.

2. *Do you need other data?* Sometimes you need to go out and get more data in order to make a stronger argument or to check your preliminary findings.

3. *Do you have the right question?* After looking at the data, is it clear that the question you tried to answer has immediate relevance. It may be more important to refine your question a bit or focus on something different. However, it the data appear appropriate for your question you can press on to the subsequent stages of the process.

Modeling

Watch a video: Framework | Associational Analyses | Prediction

What Are the Goals of Formal Modeling?

One key goal of formal modeling is to develop a precise specification of your question and how your data can be used to answer that question. Formal models allow you to identify clearly what you are trying to infer from data and what form the relationships between features of the population take. It can be difficult to achieve this kind of precision using words alone.

Parameters play an important role in many formal statistical models (in statistical language, these are known as *parametric statistical models*). These are numbers that we use to represent features or associations that exist in the population. Because they represent population features, parameters are generally considered unknown, and our goal is to estimate them from the data we collect.

For example, suppose we want to assess the relationship between the number of ounces of soda consumed by a person per day and that person's BMI. The slope of a line that you might plot visualizing this relationship is the parameter you want to estimate to answer your question: "How much would BMI be expected to increase per each additional ounce of soda consumed?" More specifically, you are using a *linear regression model* to formulate this problem.

Another goal of formal modeling is to develop a rigorous framework with which you can challenge and test your primary results. At this point in your data analysis, you've stated and refined your question, you've explored the data visually and maybe conducted some exploratory modeling. The key thing is that you likely have a pretty good sense of what the answer to your question is, but maybe have some doubts about whether your findings will hold up under intense scrutiny. Assuming you are still interested in moving forward with your results, this is where formal modeling can play an important role.

We can apply the basic epicycle of analysis to the formal modeling portion of data analysis. We still want to set expectations, collect information, and refine our expectations based on the data. In this setting, these three phases look as follows.

1. **Setting expectations**. Setting expectations comes in the form of developing a *primary model* that represents your best sense of what provides the answer to your question. This model is chosen based on whatever information you have currently available.
2. **Collecting Information**. Once the primary model is set, we will want to create a set of secondary models that challenge the primary model in some way. We will discuss examples of what this means below.
3. **Revising expectations**. If our secondary models are successful in challenging our primary model and put the primary model's conclusions in some doubt, then we may need to adjust or modify the primary model to better reflect what we have learned from the secondary models.

It's often useful to start with a *primary model*. This model will likely be derived from any exploratory analyses that you have already conducted and will serve as the lead candidate for something that succinctly summarizes your results and matches your expectations. It's important to realize that at any given moment in a data analysis, the primary model is *not necessarily the final model*. It is simply the model against which you will compare other secondary models. The process of comparing your model to other secondary models is often referred to as *sensitivity analyses*, because you are interested in seeing how sensitive your model is to changes, such as adding or deleting predictors or removing outliers in the data.

Through the iterative process of formal modeling, you may decide that a different model is better suited as the primary model. This is okay, and is all part of the process of setting expectations, collecting information, and refining expectations based on the data.

Once you have decided on a primary model, you will then typically develop a series of secondary models. The purpose of these models is to test the legitimacy and robustness of your primary model and potentially generate evidence against your primary model. If the secondary models are successful in generating evidence that refutes the conclusions of your primary model, then you may need to revisit the primary model and whether its conclusions are still reasonable.

Associational Analyses

Associational analyses are ones where we are looking at an association between two or more features in the presence of other potentially confounding factors. There are three classes of variables that are important to think about in an associational analysis.

1. **Outcome**. The outcome is the feature of your dataset
    that is thought to change along with your **key pre-
    dictor**. Even if you are not asking a causal or mech-
    anistic question, so you don't necessarily believe that
    the outcome *responds* to changes in the key predictor,
    an outcome still needs to be defined for most formal
    modeling approaches.
2. **Key predictor**. Often for associational analyses there
    is one key predictor of interest (there may be a few of
    them). We want to know how the outcome changes
    with this key predictor. However, our understanding
    of that relationship may be challenged by the presence
    of potential confounders.
3. **Potential confounders**. This is a large class of predic-
    tors that are both related to the key predictor and the
    outcome. It's important to have a good understanding
    what these are and whether they are available in your
    dataset. If a key confounder is not available in the
    dataset, sometimes there will be a proxy that is related
    to that key confounder that can be substituted instead.

Once you have identified these three classes of variables in
your dataset, you can start to think about formal modeling
in an associational setting.

This is a linear model is a common approach to quantifying
the relationship between the key predictor and the outcome
while adjusting for any potential confounders. In many
cases linear model can be used as the primary model (or at
least as a reasonable approximation). Typically you would
include the key predictor and one or a few confounders in
the model where it is perhaps well known that you should
adjust for those confounders. This model may produce
sensible results and follows what is generally known in the
area.

Secondary models for associational analyses will typically include more or more complex confounder information. Often this is because we do not know for sure whether we actually observe all of the factors that potentially confound the relationship between our outcome and key predictor. Therefore, it's sometimes helpful to include a number of additional factors tha ttest whether our primary association is very sensitive to the inclusion of those factors.

Determining where to go from here may depend on factors outside of the dataset. Some typical considerations are

1. *Effect size.* Different models may present a range of estimates. Is this a large range? It's possible that for your organization a range of this magnitude is not large enough to really make a difference and so all of the models might be considered equivalent. Or you might consider the different estimates to be significantly different from each other, in which case you might put more weight on one model over another. Another factor might be cost, in which case you would be interested in the return on your investment for whatever decision you plan to make based on this analysis.

2. *Plausibility.* Although you may fit a series of models for the purposes of challenging your primary model, it may be the case that some models are more plausible than others, in terms of being close to whatever the "truth" about the population is. Whether a model could be considered more or less plausible will depend on your knowledge of the subject matter and your ability to map real-world events to the mathematical formulation of the model. You may need to consult with other experts in this area to assess the plausibility of various models.

3. *Parsimony.* In the case where the different models all tell the same story it's often preferable to choose the model that is simplest. There are two reasons for this. First, with a simpler model it can be easier to tell a story about what is going on in the data via the various parameters in the model. For example, it's easier to explain a linear trend than it is to explain an exponential trend. Second, simpler models, from a statistical perspective, are more "efficient", so that they make better use of the data per parameter that is being estimated. Complexity in a statistical model generally refers to the number of parameters in the model. If the primary and secondary models produce significant differences, then you still might choose a parsimonious model over a more complex model, but not if the more complex model tells a more compelling story.

Prediction Analyses

In the previous section we described associational analyses, where the goal is to see if a key predictor and an outcome are associated. But sometimes the goal is to use all of the information available to you to predict the outcome. Furthermore, it doesn't matter if the variables would be considered unrelated in a causal way to the outcome you want to predict because the objective is prediction, not developing an understanding about the relationships between features.

With prediction models, we have outcome variables–features about which we would like to make predictions–but we typically do not make a distinction between "key predictors" and other predictors. In most cases, any predictor that might be of use in predicting the outcome would be considered in an analysis and might, *a priori*, be given equal weight in terms of its importance in predicting the outcome. Prediction analyses will often leave it to the prediction algorithm to determine the importance of each predictor and to determine the functional form of the model.

For many prediction analyses it is not possible to literally write down the model that is being used to predict because it cannot be represented using standard mathematical notation. Many modern prediction routines are structured as algorithms or procedures that take inputs and transform them into outputs. The path that the inputs take to be transformed into outputs may be highly nonlinear and predictors may interact with other predictors on the way. Typically, there are no parameters of interest that we try to estimate–in fact many algorithmic procedures do not have any estimable parameters at all.

The key thing to remember with prediction analyses is that we usually do not care about the specific details of the model. In most cases, as long as the method "works", is reproducible, and produces good predictions with minimal error, then we have achieved our goals.

For prediction problems, deciding on the next step after initial model fitting can depend on a few factors.

1. *Prediction quality*. Is the model's accuracy good enough for your purposes? This depends on the ultimate goal and the risks associated with subsequent actions. For medical applications, where the outcome might be the presence of a disease, we may want to have a high sensitivity, so that if you genuinely have the disease, the algorithm will detect it. That way we can get you into treatment quickly. However, if the treatment is very painful, perhaps with many side effects, then we might actually prefer a high specificity, which would

ensure that we don't mistakenly treat someone who *doesn't* have the disease. For financial applications, like the credit worthiness example used here, there may be asymmetric costs associated with mistaking good credit for bad versus mistaking bad credit for good.

2. *Model tuning.* A hallmark of prediction algorithms is their many tuning parameters. Sometimes these parameters can have large effects on prediction quality if they are changed and so it is important to be informed of the impact of tuning parameters for whatever algorithm you use. There is no prediction algorithm for which a single set of tuning parameters works well for all problems. Most likely, for the initial model fit, you will use "default" parameters, but these defaults may not be sufficient for your purposes. Fiddling with the tuning parameters may greatly change the quality of your predictions. It's very important that you document the values of these tuning parameters so that the analysis can be reproduced in the future.

3. *Availability of Other Data.* Many prediction algorithms are quite good at exploring the structure of large and complex datasets and identifying a structure that can best predict your outcome. If you find that your model is not working well, even after some adjustment of tuning parameters, it is likely that you need additional data to improve your prediction.

Formal modeling is typically the most technical aspect of data analysis, and its purpose is to precisely lay out what is the goal of the analysis and to provide a rigorous framework for challenging your findings and for testing your assumptions. The approach that you take can vary depending primarily on whether your question is fundamentally about estimating an association develoing a good prediction.

Interpretation

Watch a video: Interpretation

There are several principles of interpreting results that we will illustrate in this chapter. These principles are:

1. *Revisit your original question.* This may seem like a flippant statement, but it is not uncommon for people to lose their way as they go through the process of exploratory analysis and formal modeling. This typically happens when a data analyst wanders too far off course pursuing an incidental finding that appears in the process of exploratory data analysis or formal modeling. Then the final model(s) provide an answer to another question that popped up during the analyses rather than the original question. Revisiting your question also provides a framework for interpreting your results because you can remind yourself of the type of question that you asked.

2. Start with the primary statistical model to get your bearings and focus on the nature of the result rather than on a binary assessment of the result (e.g. statistically significant or not). The nature of the result includes three characteristics: its directionality, magnitude, and uncertainty. Uncertainty is an assessment of how likely the result was obtained by chance. eting your results will be missed if you zoom in on a single feature of your result, so that you either ignore or gloss over other important information provided by the model. Although your interpretation isn't complete until you consider the results in totality, it is often

most helpful to first focus on interpreting the results of the model that you believe best answers your question and reflects (or "fits") your data, which is your primary model. Don't spend a lot of time worrying about which single model to start with, because in the end you will consider all of your results and this initial interpretation exercise serves to orient you and provide a framework for your final interpretation.

3. *Develop an overall interpretation* based on (a) the totality of your analysis and (b) the context of what is already known about the subject matter. The interpretation of the results from your primary model serves to set the expectation for your overall interpretation when you consider all of your analyses. Recall that this primary model was constructed after gathering information through exploratory analyses and that you may have refined this model when you were going through the process of interpreting its results by evaluating the directionality, magnitude and uncertainty of the model's results. External information is both general knowledge that you or your team members have about the topic, results from similar analyses, and information about the target population.

4. Consider the implications, which will guide you in determining what action(s), if any, should be taken as a result of the answer to your question. After all, the point of doing an analysis is usually to inform a decision or to take an action. Sometimes the implications are straightforward, but other times the implications take some thought. An example of a straightforward implication is if you performed an analysis to determine if purchasing ads increased sales, and if so, did the investment in ads result in a net profit. You may learn that either there was a net profit or not, and if there were a net profit, this finding would support

continuing the ads.

Communication

Watch a video: Routine Communication | Presentations

Communication is fundamental to good data analysis. Data analysis is an inherently verbal process that requires constant discussion. What we aim to address in this chapter is the role of routine communication in the process of doing your data analysis and in disseminating your final results in a more formal setting, often to an external, larger audience. There are lots of good books that address the "how-to" of giving formal presentations, either in the form of a talk or a written piece, such as a white paper or scientific paper. In this section we will focus on how to use routine communication as one of the tools needed to perform a good data analysis how to convey the key points of your data analysis when communicating informally and formally.

Communication is both one of the tools of data analysis, and also the final product of data analysis: there is no point in doing a data analysis if you're not going to communicate your process and results to an audience. A good data analyst communicates informally multiple times during the data analysis process and also gives careful thought to communicating the final results so that the analysis is as useful and informative as possible to the wider audience it was intended for.

The main purpose of routine communication is to gather data, which is part of the epicyclic process for each core activity. You gather data by communicating your results and the responses you receive from your audience should inform the next steps in your data analysis. The types of responses you receive include not only answers to specific questions, but also commentary and questions your audience has in response to your report (either written or oral). The form that your routine communication takes depends on what the goal of the communication is. If your goal, for example, is to get clarity on how a variable is coded because when you explore the dataset it appears to be an ordinal variable, but you had understood that it was a continous variable, your communication is brief and to the point.

If, on the other hand, some results from your exploratory data analysis are not what you expected, your communication may take the form of a small, informal meeting that includes displaying tables and/or figures pertinent to your issue. A third type of informal communication is one in which you may not have specific questions to ask of your audience, but instead are seeking feedback on the data analysis process and/or results to help you refine the process and/or to inform your next steps.

In sum, there are three main types of informal communication and they are classified based on the objectives you have for the communication: (1) to answer a very focused question, which is often a technical question or a question aimed at gathering a fact, (2) to help you work through some results that are puzzling or not quite what you expected, and (3) to get general impressions and feedback as a means of identifying issues that had not occurred to you so that you can refine your data analysis.

Focusing on a few core concepts will help you achieve your objectives when planning routine communication. These concepts are:

1. **Audience**: Know your audience and when you have control over who the audience is, select the right audience for the kind of feedback you are looking for.

In some cases, such as when you are delivering an interim report to your boss or your team, the audience may be pre-determined. Your audience may be composed of other data analysts, the individual(s) who initiated the question, your boss and/or other managers or executive team members, non-data analysts who are content experts, and/or someone representing the general public.

2. **Content**: Be focused and concise, but provide sufficient information for the audience to understand the information you are presenting and question(s) you are asking.

3. **Style**: Avoid jargon. Unless you are communicating about a focused highly technical issue to a highly technical audience, it is best to use language and figures and tables that can be understood by a more general audience.

4. **Attitude**: Have an open, collaborative attitude so that you are ready to fully engage in a dialogue and so that your audience gets the message that your goal is not to "defend" your question or work, but rather to get their input so that you can do your best work.

Data Science in Real Life

If you want a condensed and fun version of this Part, you can watch this short cartoon.

What You've Gotten Yourself Into

Have you ever had the perfect data science experiment? In the perfect data science experiment,

1. You have clearly defined hypotheses that are specified a priori.
2. You're able to carefully design the experiment. For example, you can use randomization across the treatment of interest and you are aware of, can measure and can block on important confounding variables.
3. Your sample is a random sample from a population of interests so you know that your results will be generalizable.
4. The data that you have are directly able to interrogate the hypothesis that you're interested in.
5. All the data set creation and merging and data pulls from the larger data set goes smoothly.
6. There's no missing data or dropout.
7. Your analyses are robust without the need for any sort of advance modeling.
8. Your conclusions are clear and parsimonious of knowledge is gained via the experiment.
9. The decision is obvious given the data and analysis.
10. The results are communicated clearly with a nice report or data product.

Has this ever happened in real life? Probably not. (Certainly not to your authors.) In real life, often the data is needed to both inform the hypotheses and interrogate the hypotheses. Multiple comparisons are an issue because you've tried several different hypotheses or you're looking at multiple things at once.

Your access to experimental design is limited or nonexistent and you must take what you can get. The data is often completely observational with nothing intervened on or randomized. Take, for example, studying a behavior like smoking or a trait, like height. Your ability to randomize or on intervene on these factors is either not ethical or not possible.

In the terms of generalizability, the population being studied rarely is the population that you're actually interested in. In clinical trials, for example, professional "Guinea pigs" (people who frequently get paid to participate as subjects in clinical trials) are often the sample. These folks have good adherence to treatments, stay in the study the whole time and have a whole host of other behaviors unlike the real population.[1]

The data often don't have the exact measurements that you need to evaluate the hypothesis. For example, in nutrition, it's often of interest to study caloric intake. However, instead all you have are so called food frequency questionnaires where you ask people how many calories they ate last week.

Another issue arises when the data set itself is problematic. For example, merging has multiple matches, when matching should be unique or there are missing matches when every record should have a match. There can be data entry errors or errors in pulling the data from its original source. In short, the reality of building the analytic data set is a

---

[1] See this article http://www.newyorker.com/magazine/2008/01/07/guinea-pigging

challenging process.

A frequent problem with experimental and observational data is missingness, which often requires advanced modeling to address. And then because you need advanced modeling, advanced computing is needed to fit the model, which raises issues with robustness and bugs.

When you're all done with this messy process, often your conclusions wind up being indeterminate and the decision is not substantially further informed by the data and the models that you've fit.

Maybe all of these things don't happen at once, but at least some of them or others do in most data science experiments.

Let's go through some examples of these problems that we've seen recently.

Data double duty

As an example, our colleagues wrote this wonderful paper about, exactly about the issue of using your data to come up with your hypotheses. They work in the area of multiple sclerosis (MS). A common problem in the area of MS brain research with magnetic resonance imaging is actually defining what it means for a lesion to be so-called "enhancing", which is an imaging indicator of a progessively worsening lesion. However, there was no clear way to quantitatively define a lesion as enhancing and they were usually diagnosed by having a radiologist look at it. They put forward a framework that both quantitatively identified the hypotheses and interrogated the hypotheses with the same data set. Such analyses are tremendously prone to errors of getting biased results comparing the hypotheses.

Since they're statistical researchers so their emphasis was on doing this in a rigorous fashion to avoid such errors. However, it's an example of a setting where the hypotheses wasn't specified ahead of time and the data had to perform double duty where a great deal of sophistication is necessary to avoid spurious conclusions.

Multiplicity

Multiple comparisons. Since we're on the subject of brain imaging, which is the area that I work on, multiple comparisons is often an issue. And in one particularly famous example, some people put a dead salmon in an fMRI machine to detect brain activation. Of course, there's no brain activation in a dead salmon. What they've found is that if you do lots and lots and lots of tests, and you don't account for that correctly, you can see brain activation in a dead salmon.

Randomization versus observational studies

A very famous example of randomization was from the Women's Health Initiative. The Women's Health initiative conducted a study, a randomized trial of hormone replacement therapy, which at the time, was a fairly standard treatment for post menopausal women. The results of these randomized trials contradicted what was thought of as common knowledge for the advocacy of hormone replacement therapy and the safety of it. And so it brought about a lot of soul searching about the value of a randomized trial versus the value of a lot of observational data. And I think it's maybe not necessary to go into the weeds of this study for the purposes of this chapter. However, suffice it to say, the randomized trial carried a lot of weight with it because of the randomization. All the previous observational trials where they just saw whether or not women were on hormone replacement therapy and watched them over time. The multitude of those studies was not deemed as rigorous as the one study that had randomization where women were actually randomized to hormone replacement therapy or not. And as a side note, if you're interested about reading up on hormone replacement therapy. I put a website here from the Women's Health Initiative where you can actually go and look on the frequently asked questions relating to some of the studies that have done since then. There's been a decade of work since then that further refine the science on this particular issue. The main point for this lecture is the importance, how important randomization was in this particular setting.

In this chapter, we'll contrast data science in the ideal versus data science in real life. We'll discuss different variations of experimental design versus observational studies and how you can check for errant data and other tools to make data analysis in real life a little bit more manageable.

The Data Pull is Clean

Lecture slides

In real life, data can be very messy. In this chapter, when we talk about the data pull, we're talking about all the different components that go into going from raw data into an analytic data set. In this process, several intermediate steps are required.

First, one typically has to arrange the analytic data set from a larger more complex data source (data pull). In addition, it is often required to merge disparate sorts of data, resulting in matching errors. For example, in a analysis that I (Brian) worked on, I had to connect insurance claims with individual data. There were claims with no matching individual, individuals with no claims, and presumably mismatches of other sorts. Presumably there were also errant claim IDs that resulted in apparent correct matches with indidividuals, with no fullproof way to diagnose such matching errors.

Another frequent issue in creating an analytic data set is in summarizing complex data types. For example, you might have recorded voice data or text data that you need to convert into meaningful summaries. In the area that I work in, interest lies in large, complex, brain imaging data. Summarizing those down into a handful of numbers that represent certain regions of the brain is a complex process that is frought with errors and complexities.

Another very common problem is going from data that is convenient for one purpose into a convenient form for analysis. In other words, the way we might store the data for archival purposes is generally not what's right for analysis purposes. This can be as simple as compressed data, but is often more complicated. The brain imaging data mentioned earlier is often stored in 3D or 4D (fourth dimension being time) arrays, which typically not the best format for analysis. Other examples include: language data being converted into n-grams, fine scale (minute, second, nanosecond) stock values converted into coarser (daily or monthly) values and so on. This process of converting often introduces errors or unanticipated loss of information.

As a manager, you're probably not going to actually execute any of the necessary coding. Maybe you did that in your past, but now you're managing groups of people or individuals that are doing this for you. While there's tons of generic tools to protect coders from errors, there aren't that many tools to help managers help the people they're managing. So we give some simple tools that can help ensure data quality in real life.

The first thing worth mentioning is the simple act of creating what I like to call Table 1. Table 1. is basically a summary table of interest and, surprisingly, these are a great way to catch errors. The phrase Table 1. comes from scientific papers where the first table is almost always just a summary table of demographics and basic information.

These basic summary tables are a great way to catch errors. A group of people with fresh eyes thinking high level about basic summaries spot odd things that easily get lost for the analyst that is neck deep in the weeds of data analysis. An important consideration is to get standard deviations along with means, medians and quantiles. Also refer back to old tables as you meet with your team recurrently. Jumps in quantities that should be stable are a great way to catch data errors. Another important one is to check your units. By this, I mean your scientific units (inches, pounds, hits). It's a good habit to attach units to everything and actively discuss the units. As an example, if you have errant data that would suggest too many clicks per second, but everyone assumes the data are in clicks per minute, an obvious error might go unnoticed. Force the discussion by requiring units to be explicit.

After you've done some regression modeling, regression diagnostics are an extremely useful way to detect data errors. My favorite examples of regression diagnostics are from Len Stefansky from North Carolina State. He creates data for students where scatter plots appear normal, but residual plots show interesting pictures, like Homer Simpson or text that says "check your residuals". This is his way of showing how residual plots can highlight hidden systematic patterns in our data. http://www4.stat.ncsu.edu/~stefanski/NSF_-Supported/Hidden_Images/stat_res_plots.html

Of course, residual plots are only useful after you've done your modeling. Given that this is the case, there's a few other regression diagnostics you might consider. We'll give some basic definitions:

Residuals are the difference between the response (the outcome that you're studying) and the fitted value (what your model predicts it would be). When looking at residuals make sure that there aren't any systematic patterns or extremely large values that are well outside the general pattern.

hat values or **hat diagonals**, and they consider how variable a data row of explanatory variable is among its space of fellow predictors. So hat values help you tell how outside of the normal range of variability, this particular row of data is.

dffits, **dfbetas**, and **Cook's distance** are all related statistical measures. These measures all compare some aspect of the model from the fit the model with a point deleted and the model with that point included. For example, if you compare the fitted values with the data point deleted and included in the fit, you get the dffits. If you compare the slope estimates then you get what are called the dfbetas. If you compare the slope estimates aggregated into one single number, one single metric called Cook's distance (named after its inventor). All of these are influence measures. They're trying to do is tell you how much did things change when a data row is deleted from model fitting. They're almost always introduced primarily for considering model fit. However, not only do they help you evaluate things about your regression model, they also help you perform data quality control.

Another fascinating way to consider data quality is Benford's law. This is a phenomenological law about leading digits. It can sometimes help with data entry errors. For example, if those doing the data entry like to systematically round down when they shouldn't.

The final thing you might want to try is actually checking specific rows of your data through so-called data quality queries, DQQs. Of course you can't check every single point; however, you can check some. And you can use statistical procedures, like random sampling, to get a random sample of rows of your data, check those rows individually. Because it's a nice random sample, you can get an estimate of the proportion of bad rows in your data.

The Experiment is Carefully Designed: Principles

Lecture notes for this chapter:

- Introductory video
- Causality

In this chapter consider the difference between statistically designed and observational studies.

An experimentally designed study is the case where you have tight control over several aspects of the experiment. Good experimental design can do things like account for known important factors through things like blocking and stratification. In addition, it can account for unknown confounding factors through randomization. Experimental design can help in the terms of bias by random sampling. If you execute good experimental design and everything goes well, often it eliminates the need for complex analyses. Simple analysis usually suffice, and are better in these settings. Carfully designed experiments help us isolate the effects of interest.

More often we have an observational experiment. This is the opposite setting, where you don't have tight control over the experiment or sample. In an observational experiment, you're collecting it as or after it occurs without interventions. This has some benefits as well. For example, it's often feasible when designed experiments are not. You can't, for example, ethically randomize people in a study of smoking behaviors. In addition, observational studies often have very large sample sizes since passive monitoring or retrospective data collection is typically much cheaper than active intervention.

On the negative side, in order to get things out of observational data analysis, you often need much more complex modeling and assumptions, because you haven't been able to do things, like control for known important factors as part of the design. Thus, it's almost always the case that an observational study needs larger sample sizes to accommodate the much more complex analysis that you have to do to study them.

In the next few sections, we'll cover some of the key aspects and considerations of designed and observational experiments.

Causality

"Correlation isn't causation" is one of the most famous phrases about statistics. However, why collect the data or do the study if we can never figure out cause? For most people, the combination of iterating over the empirical evidence, the scientific basis, face validity and the assumptions eventually establishes causality. Relatively recent efforts from statisticians, economists, epidemiologists and others have formalized this process quite a bit. One aspect is that good experimental design can get us closer to a causal interpretation with fewer assumptions.

However, to make any headway on this problem, we have to define causation, which we will do with so-called counterfactuals. The philosopher David Hume codified this way of thinking about causality, which is the only one we consider in this book. There are many others.

In a statistical sense, a **counterfactual** is an outcome that would have occurred a different set of conditions than actually happened (i.e. counter to the facts of what actually occurred). For example, if a subject receives an experimental medication, their counterfactual would be their outcome had they not received the treatment, with all else being held the same. For a subject that didn't receive the treatment, the counterfactual would be the their outcome had they received it. The counterfactual difference (also often just referred to as the counterfactual) is the difference between the two. In our example, it's the difference between the outcome that was observed and the outcome that would have been observed if the subject received the opposite treatment.

This difference define the counterfactual causal effect of the treatment on a subject: the change in the outcome from the treatment that the subject actually received and what would've occurred had she or he received the other treatment.

Thus our causal effect requires something observe with something we *cannot* observe.

Let's go through a conceptual example. Just to frame an example that everyone would have familiarity with, let's discuss an exercise regimen. In the video lectures, I consider a silly exercise called the Twist and Tone. A person can only either be using the Twist and Tone or not. Let's assume that the outcome of interest was weight loss. The causal effect would be difference in weight loss or gain between from the subject using the Twist and Tone program to not using it, with all else being the same.

We cannot observe, at the same time, a person who has both

used the Twist and Tone and not used the Twist and Tone. We could, however, look at a person before they used it, then afterwards. This would not be at the same time and any effect we saw could be aliased with time. For example, if the subject was measured before the holidays not using the Twist and Tone, the counterfactual difference in weight gain/loss could just be due to holiday weight gain. We'll come back to designs like this later. Suffice it to say that we can't actually get at the causal effect for an individual, without untestable and unreasonable assumptions. However we can get at, we can estimate the average causal effect, the average of counterfactual differences across individuals, under some reasonable assumptions under certain study designs.

The average causal effect (ACE) isn't itself a counterfactual difference, it's an estimate of the average of counterfactual differences obtained when you only get to see subjects under one treatment. The simplest way to obtain this estimate is with randomziation. So, for example, if we were to randomize the Twist and Tone to half of our subjects and a control regimen to the other half, the average difference in weight loss would be thought of as the ACE.

You can think of the ACE as a "policy effect". It estimates what the impact of enacting the Twist and Tone exercise regimen as a matter of policy across subjects similar to the ones in our study would be. It does not say that the Twist and Tone will have a good counterfactual difference for every subject. In other words, causal thinking in this way is not "mechanistic thinking". If you want to understand mechanisms, you have to take a different approach. However, thinking causally this way is incredibly useful for fields like public health, where many of the issues are policies. For example: "Would the hosptial infection rate decline after the introduction of a hand washing program?",

"Would childhood obesity decline if laws were enacted to prevent soda beverage machines in lunchrooms?", "Would heart attacks decline if indoor smoking bans were enacted?".

There are some important considerations when thinking about causality. Use of randomization is the best way to get at the ACE. However, generalizability is separate issue. Even with randomization, if your subjects are fundamentally different than the ones you'd like to generalize to, your ACE estimator isn't very useful. We'll talk more about this in the bias section.

Another consideration is that your treatment has to be conceptually assignable to think about causal inference in this way. For example, your eye color isn't assignable (can't be randomized). The treatments have to be stable in the sense that a subject's treatment status doesn't impact another's outcome. You can think of things like vaccine trials and transmission where this would fail to be true.

A final consideration. Without explicit randomization, one must make more assumptions to estimate the ACE that are beyond the scope of this book. Students interested in causal inference should consider reading one of the many introductory books devoted to the topic.

Crossover trials

For example, consider crossover trials. In these experiments, a subject is given a treatment, then there's a washout period, then they're given the control (or vice versa). Usually which they receive first is randomized. What assumptions would be necessary for the subject differences to look like a counterfactual difference? Would this design work for a trial of teaching methods? Would it work for a headache medication? Try to think about these questions now with some of the causal ideas in mind!

Natural experiments

Let's consider another way of analyzing and thinking about analysis using natural experiments. Again, I'd like you to use your new knowledge of thinking in the terms of causal effects when thinking about these kinds of analyses.

A great example of natural experiments is where smoking bans were enacted. You can't randomize smoking status to see whether smoking is a causal factor in heart attacks. What you can look at are places that put in smoking bans before and after the ban went into effect and look at hosptialization records for heart attacs at the same times. However, if that same election cycle had other policies that also impacted things, those other policies could also be the cause of whatever decline in cardiac issues that you saw from your hospital records. The same can be said for anything else that is similarly aliased with timing of the bans.

Naturalized natural experiments study the impact of an external manipulation, like a ban going into effect, to try to get at causality, with a lot of assumptions.

Matching

Matching is this idea of finding dopplegangers.
If I have a collection of subjects that received the treatment, for each one I find a control subjects who is very close in every other respect (dopplegangers). Then I analyze these pairs of dopplegangers. This is very commonly done in medical studies. A classic example is lung cancer studies of smoking. If you have historical smoking status and other information of a collection of subjects who were diagnosed with lung cancer, you could find a set of similar in all relevant aspects subjects without lung cancer then comparing the smoking rates between the groups. Hopefully, you see how the matching connects to our idea of trying to get at counterfactual differences and how looking backward is

certainly going to be a lot easier than following smokers up for decades to see if they eventually get cancer.f Hopefully you also see the many flaws in this study design. A big one is the issue that you may have forgotten to match on an important variable, or matched on one that was unimportant, but highly correlated with smoking status. The retrospective design has issues as well, such as with generalizability and the necessary assumptions.

Randomization is our best tool for finding average causal effects. We'll discuss more in the lecture on randomization in AB testing. So what are some other examples of things we can do when don't have randomization? Perhaps the most common way is to use some sort of modeling. Methods such as propensity scores and others rely on developing accurate models of treatment assignment. Others, like natural experiments and instrumental variables require a degree of luck and cleverness that doesn't lend itself well to general application. However, every method will come with its assumptions and limitations. The modern study of causal inference focuses on elucidating the assumptions and limitations and making as robust inferences as possible. I hope that this chapter has inspired enough of an interest in causal inference ideas for further reading and hopefully use in your data science management.

Confounding

One aspect of analysis is so persistent that it deserves repeated mention throughout this chapter and that is of confounding. If you want a simple rule to remember confounding by it's this: *The apparent relationship or lack of relationship between A and B may be due to their joint relationship with C.* Many examples of controversial or hotly argued statistical relationships boil down to this statement. To mention some famous ones: *The apparent relationship between lung cancer and smoking may be due to their joint relationship in genetics* (a historically famous example). *The apparent relationship between man made carbon emissions and global average temperature is due to their joint relationship with natural carbon emissions. The apparent relationship between the race of murder trial defendants and a death penalty sentence is due to their joint relationship with the race of the victims.*

Let's go through a simple exam that Jeff concocted just to illustrate the principle of confounding. Here we see a picture of Jeff playing with his son. Jeff points out that he has big shoes, and he's literate. His son has little shoes and is not literate. If you were to collect a large dataset of fathers and sons, you would find the relationship was statistically significant. Of course, we would all agree that the confounding variable in this case is age. In other words, *the apparent relationship between literacy and shoe size is due to their joint relationship with age.*

Addressing known confounders is at least conceptually easy. For example, if one were to account for age in the analysis, such as looking within age groups, you would find no apparent relationship between shoe size and literacy rate. However, common issues are the existence of too many confounders to address or unobserved or unknown confounders that should be addressed.

One can also adress confounders at the design phase. We'll discuss this more in the next section on A/B testing.

The Experiment is Carefully Designed: Things to Do

Lecture ntoes for this section:

- A/B Testing
- Sampling
- Adjustment / blocking

A/B testing

A/B testing is the use of randomized trials in data science settings. To put this in context, let's consider two ad campaigns that Jeff is using to sell books. Let's say campaign A and B, respectively. How would one evaluate the campaigns?

One could run the ads serially; he could run ad A for a couple of weeks then ad B for a couple of weeks, and then compare the conversion rate during the time periods of the two ads. Under this approach, anything relationship found could be attributed to whatever's aliased with the time periods that he was studying. For example, imagine if the first ad ran during Christmas or a major holiday. Then, of course people's purchasing patterns are different during that time of year. So any observed difference could be attributed to the unlucky timing of the ads.

If he were to run the ads at the same time, but ran the ads on sites with different audience demographics, one wouldn't be able to differentiate ad type and audience characteristics. Ideally, he would be able to randomize across time and/or sites. This of course, doesn't guarantee that the timing or sites the ads appeared on are well balanced on all potential lurking or confounding variables. An argument could be made that better strategies exist for known confounders that would force balance. However, randomization is certainly the best strategy for trying to acheive such balance for unknown lurking variables.

Our discussion of A/B testing focuses on randomization. However, the eventual analysis can get quite challenging despite the help of randomization. As an example, how can we be sure that Jeff's ads aren't be viewed by the same people who visit different sites? If enough such people were contributing to the converion rates, indepence assumptions usually made during analyses would be incorrect. Missing or incomplete data often plague trials and A/B tests.

Sampling

It's important not to confuse randomization, a strategy used to combat lurking and confounding variables and random sampling, a stategy used to help with generalizability. In many respects generalizability is the core of what statistics is trying to accomplish, making inferences about a population from a sample. In general, it's not enough to just say things about our sample. We want to generalize that knowledge beyond our sample; a process called statistical inference.

A famous example of bias came from the so-called Kinsey Report of human sexuality. The study subjects involved many more people with psychological disorders and prisoners than were represented in the broader population.

Thus, the main criticism of the work was that it wasn't generalizable because of the importance differences between the sample and the group inferences would like to be drawn on. It's interesting to note that Kinsey's response was to simply collect more of the same kind ofsubjects, which, of course doesn't solve the problem. Simply getting a larger biased sample doesn't correct the bias.

In the terms of solutions, three strategies should be considered first. The first is random sampling where we try to draw subjects randomly from the population that we're interested in. This can often be quite hard to do. For example, in election polling, there's an entire science devoted to getting accurate polling data.

What if random sampling isn't available? Weighting is another strategy that has many positive aspects, though also some down sides. The idea of weighting is multiply observations in your sample so that they represent the population you're interested in. Imagine you wanted to estimate the average height. However, in your sample you have twice as many men as you have women. In the population that you're interested in, there's equal numbers of men and women. In weighting, you would upweight the collection of women that you had or downweight the collection of men. Thus, as far as the weighted inferences were concerned, the women and men had equal numbers. Weighting requires that you know the weights, usually based on population demographics. Moreover, certain weighting strategies can result in huge increases in the variability of estimates.

The last strategy is modeling. That is to build up a statistical model hoping that the model relationship holds outside of where you have data. This approach has the problem of actually having to build the model and whether or not our conclusions are robust to this model building. A careful

design with random sampling results in analyses that are robust to assumptions, whereas modeling can often be fraught
with errors from assumption.

Blocking and Adjustment

Imagine if you're interested in improving mobility among
the elderly using fitness tracker, say FitBit. You plan on
doing a clinical trial where you randomize half of your
subjects to receive a Fitbit, while the others get nothing.
(Side note, control subjects often get the treatment at the
end of the trial to reward them for participation.)

You are concerned that age confounds the relationship between fitness tracker usage and mobility. It's likely that the
age groups would be distributed In roughly equal propor-
tions among the treated and the controls due to the randomization. However, if you have a smaller study, chance
imbalances could occur. Because you know age is such an
important factor, you might wanna force it to be balanced
between your treated and control groups. To do this you
might want to randomize within age blocks; this is called
blocking. In other words, if you hvae a factor that you know
is important, why randomize and hope for the best?

Let's consider the same issue when you don't have control
over the experiment, or you've conducted the experiment
and realize that there was an imbalance of ages between
the treated and control groups. Focus on the observational
case where you don't have control over the experiment.
Consider studying elderly subjects comparing the use of fitness trackers with mobility. But, you are just observing the
collection of people who self-select into using fitness trackers versus the controls. Because it's an observation study,
you're worried about lots of factors that might confound the

relationship between mobility and use of a fitness tracker. However, you're very concerned about age in specific, so let's focus on that one variable. (In a typical observational study, we'd be concerned about lots of things of course.) The younger subjects are going to be more likely to use and directly engage with the features of a fitness tracker, just because of familiarity with technology. A direct comparison between fitness tracker users and controls would clearly be inappropriate. The most common solution to this problem is adjustment.

Adjustment is the idea of looking at the relationship within levels of the confounder held fixed. Consider dividing age into say five categories. A simple adjustment strategy would compare the mobility within each age category, so we're more probably comparing like with like. We may not have equal or consistent numbers of fitness tracker users and non-users within or across age groups. But, by comparing within age groups, we wouldn't be worried that our results were due to age.

There's lots of different ways to do adjustment. Perhaps the most common and easiest one is regression adjustment. In this form of adjustment we would add age into a regression model that included fitness tracker useage. The estimate with age in the model would be the adjusted estimate. This performs a model based adjustment that requires some assumptions to be effective.

Results of the Analysis Are Clear

Lecture notes:

- Multiple comparisons
- Effect sizes
- Comparing to known effects
- Negative controls

Multiple comparisons

One way results can appear unclear is if results don't paint a compelling narrative. This can happen if spurious effects are detected or too many effects are significant. A common reason for this to happen is from multiplicity.

Multiplicity is the concern of repeatedly doing hypothesis tests until one comes up significant by chance. This sounds nefarious, and it can be, but it can be often done with the best of intentions, especially in modern problems. Moreover, multiple comparisons issues can creep into analyses in unexpected ways. For example, multiple testing issues can arise from fitting too many models or from looking at too many quantities of interest within a model. The worst version of multiple comparisons is if an unscrupulous researcher keeps looking at effects until he or she finds one that is signficant then presents results as if that was the only test performed. (One could consider this less of a multiplicity problem than an ethics problem.) Of course,

most data scientists don't approach their work so poorly.
In many cases large numbers of tests are done as part of a
legitimate and honest hypothesis generating exercise. Or,
large numbers of models are fit as part of a legitimate model
building exercise.

There is a vast literature on multiple comparisons, but the
easiest fix uses an inequality that's named after the mathe-
matician, Bonferroni. Because it's named after his inequality, it's called the "Bonferroni correction". The easiest way to
execute a Bonferroni correction is to simply multiply your
P-values by the number of tests that you're performing. So,
for example, if you perform 10 tests and one of the P-values
is 0.01, then that P-value is now 0.10. You then perform your
inference as usual. This method shows you the impact of
performing more tests. If you double your number of tests,
then you have to double your P-values.

The Bonferroni correction is highly robust and it works in
all circumstances. One issue is that it can be
quite conservative. So the result of the Bonferroni correction is that it tends errs on the side of declaring effects not
significant.

A second issue with Bonferroni (and all other) corrections
is that they don't give guidance on what constitutes the
set of tests to include. That is, what number to multiply
your P-values by. The mathematics unfortunately can't help
this question. As an example, imagine that you're looking
at engagement statistics by web site design and find some
interesting positive results for a new design. You double
check your results by running the same analysis comparing
old designs you know not to be fundamentally different
and find nothing significant, as you would expect. Certainly
you shouldn't penalize your original analysis by verifying
it with a second confirmatory analysis? This is clearly a

different mind set then what we're trying to control for with multiplicity. Thus, unfortunately, there's no simple rules as to what goes into multiplicity corrections and one must appeal to reasonableness and common sense.

Effect sizes, significance, modeling

In every statistics course ever taught, this phrase is covered: *statistical significance is not practical significance.* This draws a discussion of the fact that just by reasons of having a large sample size you can detect miniscule, practically unimportant, effects. I think the picture is a lot more complicated than this simple phrase and idea suggests. In this section we discuss these more complex instances. What does it mean to get a significant or a non significant result in hypothesis testing.

What does a marginal signficiance imply?

Let's go through some thought experiments. Imagine that a very large epidemiological study of nutrition finds a slightly significant result, P-value of 0.049 associating hot dog consumption to colorectal cancer incidence. This is right under what is the typical standard of significance. So the question I would ask to you is does the larger sample size bolster the evidence or hinder it? In one sense the larger sample implies more evidence. On the other hand, why did it take such a large sample size only to get a barely significant effect?

Let's consider another similar thought experiment. A well done A/B test, with a reasonable sample size, no missing data or other complexities, finds one ad campaign is not significantly better than another; the P-value is just above the standard threshold for significance. Does the good study design bolster confidence in the lack of significance or not?

If this seems confusing, it's because it is confusing. These questions don't have a consistent answer among researchers who study problems like this!

One point worth emphasizing is that we cannot simply interpret the result of hypothesis test outside of the context. In other words, P-values and the results of hypothesis tests are not portable across settings. They're not as well calibrated across settings as we would hope.

Effect sizes

Another consideration is that the size of the effect matters. The size of the effect is often lost when you just report the result of a hypothesis test or the P-value by itself. Thus, when you're managing people, force them to report effects and relative effect sizes in addition to the results of their hypothesis tests and P-values. Confidence intervals help with this greatly, as they at least put the inference back into the units of the problem. This doesn't eliminate the need to consider context, as what constitutes a large effect in an A/B test and a large observational epidemiological study may be dramatically different. However, it gives you more relevant information to interpret in context.

Calibrating error rates

You might also ask level of error is tolerable? If you're in a circumstance where you're testing between two policies, each equally viable a priori, and you have to make a decision between the two regardless. Here, you can tolerate a high error level. Since you have to implement one or the other, so the most important consideration is making a decision. Unless the evidence is perfectly equivocal, you're gonna take evidence slightly in favor of A and go with A, or evidence slightly in favor of B and go with B. Contrast this with the error rates for a regulatory agency like the Food and Drug Administration. They have to prevent dangerous and ineffective drugs from going to market. Therefore, they put very high scrutiny on the amount of information and evidence required. They'd rather error on the side of not approving an effective drug than risk approving an ineffective one. So the standard of evidence is very different than in our earlier setting. So the result of a hypothesis test just can't be interpreted in the same way.

What biases are likely present

Another relevant consideration is what biases are likely present?
If you have a giant sample that's very biased, then you might be finding an effect, but that effect may just be detecting that bias.

Summary

Hypothesis testing is a tool that rarely should be used in isolation. If you're managing someone and they're just reporting P-values by themselves or the result of hypothesis test, you need to push them to go further. Push them to give you effect sizes; push them to give you confidence intervals; push them to put the results into the proper context of what's being studied and to contrast the results with other related studies.

Comparison with benchmark effects

In this section, we talk about ways to help us interpret effects when we're studying something that we don't know too well. The idea is simply to compare things with benchmark effects. The context we're considering is when it's hard to interpret an effect or its magnitude, because it's a newly studied phenomenon. A solution is to compare effects or significance levels with known effects.

My colleague (Brian Schwartz) and I studied past occupational lead exposure on brain volume. My colleague found an unadjusted effect estimate of -1.141 milliliters of brain volume lost per 1 microgram of lead per gram of bone mineral increase. This is hard thing to interpret. However, it might be easier to consider when we relate it to normal age related brain volume loss. Normal aging, over the age of 40 say, results in about a half a percent of decline in brain volume per year. If I take that half a percent decline in brain volume per year, and I look at the average brain volume from my colleague's study, I can figure out that 1.41 ml decrease is roughly equivalent to about about one would lose in 20% of the year in normal aging. Then I could multiply appropriately if I wanted to increase the amount of lead exposure being considered, so that 5 units of lead exposure is roughly equivalent to an extra year of normal aging.

This technique is very powerful and it can be used in many ways. Here are some (made up) examples just to give you further of an idea: *the P-value for comparing this new ad campaign to our standard is 0.01. That's twice as small as the same P-value for the ad that was so successful last year. The effect of a year of exposure to this airborn pollutant on lung cancer incidence is equivalent to 20 years of heavy cigarette smoking.*

Negative controls

Recall we're concerned with unclear results and we're giving some strategies for interogating them. In this section, we're concerned with significant effects that arose out of elaborate processing settings. Often in these settings, one is often concerned whether the process somehow created the significance spuriously. This often happens in technological research areas. In genomics, running groups of samples together creates spurious effects. In brain imaging, physiological noise creates seemingly real, but actually uninteresting effects.

So now you're worried that your results are more due to process than a real effect. How do you check? First, there's all of the regular protections of statistical inference. However, you'd like to make sure in a more data centric way that doesn't require as many assumptions. The idea is to perform a negative control experiment. You repeat the analysis for a variable that is known to have no association. In brain imaging, we often do this with the ventricles, areas inside the skull with no brain, only cerebrospinal fluid. We know that we can't see brain activation there, since there's no brain there!

In general, what are the characteristics of a good negative control? Well, they're variables that are otherwise realistic, but known to have no association with the outcome. So in our brain imaging case, they looked at something that was in the image already and was subject to all the same processing experience of the rest of the image. The main issue with negative controls is that it's often very hard to find something where you know for sure there can't possibly be an effect.

Another strategy that people employ rather than negative controls, is permutation tests. They actually break the association by permuting one of the variables. Since you'd be concerned about what if you got a chance permutation that could fool you, you look at lots of them. This is a bit more of an advance of a topic, but the idea is quite similar negative controls.

To sum up, if you're feeling queasy about the consequences of a complicated set of data munging and analysis and several models being built, repeat the whole process for something that can't possibly exhibit an association, and see what comes out. At the minimum, it's a great way to offer a sanity check, and to check influences due to process.

The Decision is Obvious

Lecture notes:

- The decision is not obvious
- Estimation target is relevant

The decision is (not) obvious

Things are easy if your tests are highly non-significant or highly significant. But what if they are right in between? We touched on marginal effects before. But now we'd like to devote a little more space to the general concept of what to do when the results of the test are just on the margin?

What are you most concerned with with a marginal effect? Probably foremost on your mind should be the idea of power. Namely, was the study set up in the first place to really adjudicate whether or not there was an effect.

Power is the probability of detecting an effect that is truly there. You want more power in a study. Okay, studies that have a larger sample size have more power than otherwise similar studies a smaller sample size. Studies that are trying to detect a bigger effect have more power than otherwise similar studies trying to detect a smaller effect. In other words, it's easier to spot an elephant than it is to spot a mouse. More error variablity in the system that you're studying, the less power you will have to detect a signal in all that noise.

After a study was conducted and has marginal results, the first question to ask was: was the power adequate, or at least having the discussion of whether this study was really set up for success. Unfortunately, post hoc, there's not that much that can be done about power. The obvious thing, collecting more data or doing another study, is usually not feasible. Calculating power after the study has been done is known to be a biased, error prone process. If you're doing this you need to be very sophisticated in the field of statistics and aware of the issues.

Because of this, in many cases all that you're left with is a critical discussion of the strength of the study. Ask questions like the following. Is the sample size similar to what was used in other studies where an effect was seen? Is the effect size relevant? Can you point to aspects of the study that may have led to the marginal results, like missing data? This kind of critical review is an important part of understanding an equivocal result and making decisions based off of it.

Estimation target is relevant

A common issue is that in either predictors or outcomes, we haven't measured the variable of interest, we've measured a surrogate. Some classic examples include body mass index as a measure of body fat percentage, GDP as a measure of national economic well-being and food frequency questionnaires for calorie consumptions.

First, we should consider the hallmarks of good surrogate variables. The best surrogates are gonna be unbiased. That is, they're not systematically different than the variable of interest. Ideally they have a known variance around the desired outcome. Consider weight obtained with an unbiased scale. If you have a scale that's kind of noisy, but its average difference from the truth is zero. Then you can use that information in your analysis without much trouble. If you know the variance, all the better and you can likely do something quite formal in your analysis.

A second very good setting is where you have the truth and the surrogate measured on some subset of the people and you can study and understand some amount of calibration. Consider activity monitors, like FitBits. These devices counts steps and calories expended, when they're actually measuring acceleration. If studying activity, one could count exact steps and calories in a lab for a subset of subjects to help calibrate in a larger study. You could use the gold standard data to understand the measurement variability and bias and use that variability and bias in your analyses.

Another reasonable strategy is to use sensitivity analysis to consider bias and variability of your surrogate variable. That is, come up with some idea of how off your individual measurements will be and then factor that into the analysis. Another cool ideas is to add more measurement variation to your variables, just by adding random normals to your data, for example, and seeing the consquence. You can increase the variance and bias of the additional measurement error this way and see what impact it has. A generalization of this idea is the so called simulation extrapolation (SimEx) method. SimEx and other methods are beyond the scope of this book. The interested reader should consider looking into surrogate variables and measurement error models for further reading.

Finally, it's worth discussing when to throw in the towel. If the variable that you're going to use in lieu of the one that you really want is so unknown and unreliable an estimate of the desired outcome that no results would change your decision or state of knowledge, then why bother running the analysis at all? Certainly goes through this exercise before conducting the study or doing the analysis.

Analysis Product is Awesome

Lecture notes:

- Reproducibility
- Version control

In this chapter we consider the products of the analysis. This is usually some sort of report or presentation. If the analysis is far enough along, then it might be an app or web page. We have a coursera class exactly on topic of the technical development of data products.

If the product is a report, ideally, it would clear and concisely written, with a nice narrative and interesting results. However, the needs of data science managers are variable enough that we focus on two components that make for good final products that are ubiquitous across all settings. These are making the report reproducible and making the report and code version controlled.

Analysis reproducible considers the fact that if we ask people to replicate their own analysis, let alone someone else's, they often get different results, sometimes, very different. We have a coursera class on making reproducible reports. The benefits of using the right tools for reproducible reports are many. They include dramatically helping achieve the goal of reproducibility, but also: helping organize ones thinking by blending the code and the narrative into a single document, they help document the code in a way that commenting doesn't achieve and they help automate the report writing process.

Thus if you're managing data scientists, we suggest knitr and iPython notebooks. These tools knit the analysis and the report together. And they're easy to learn.

As for the content of the report, some other recommendations that come to mind.

Check the signs, magnitudes and units. Checking the signs means checking that your effects are in the direction that you expect. It's also helps enforce asking the people that you manage to do more than just reporting coefficients. Checking the magnitudes by comparison with other known effects (covered in an earlier lecture) is a really good thing to encourage. Finally, put units on everything (graph axes, coefficients, means, ...) And make sure to understand the units. I can't tell you how many times this small step has helped.

It's important to get the data scientists and analysts that you mange out of technical jargon speak and into interpretation and interpretability. For the former, I keep harping on this idea of comparison with other known effects. Secondly, I encourage the idea of effect critiquing. This is the idea of, instead of getting excited about an effect, become its biggest critic. Try to figure out every possible reason why it could be spurious. This almost always leads to new analysis that should be conducted. Finally, for interpretability, encourage parsimonious models with interpretable parameters. That is, place a premium on simplicity. This is, of course, if you're more interested in a data science experiment where you are trying to create new parsimonious knowledge. The situation changes if one is trying to only improve prediction (see the first lecture).

Finally, version control is just general good practice. Version control is the process of keeping versions of your software, code, data and reports. Modern version control software makes this process easy. Using good version control, the project can be reverted to any previous step, and all of the steps are commented. Tools like git make this possible in massively distributed settings where lots of people are working on the same project. Git is the version control software, and a git repository is the actual version control database. Collaboration on a git repository occurs on a server. Fortunately, there are tons of hosted git servers out there for general and business use. The biggest one is GitHub though others like bitbucket are also great. These offer nice web interfaces to the server as well. There's an entire free book on git and a million tutorials online.

Of course, git is one of many version control systems. The main point is recommend (or demand/force) a version control culture in your organization.

About the Authors

Brian Caffo is a Professor in the Department of Biostatistics at the Johns Hopkins University Bloomberg School of Public Health. He co-leads a working group, www.smartstats.org, that focuses on the statistical analysis of imaging and biosignals. He is the recipient of the Presidential Early Career Award for Scientists and Engineers and was named a fellow of the American Statistical Association.

Roger D. Peng is a Professor of Biostatistics at the Johns Hopkins Bloomberg School of Public Health. He is also a Co-Founder of the Johns Hopkins Data Science Specialization, the Johns Hopkins Executive Data Science Specialization, the Simply Statistics blog where he writes about statistics and data science for the general public, and the Not So Standard Deviations podcast. Roger can be found on Twitter and GitHub under the user name @rdpeng.

Jeffrey T. Leek is an Associate Professor of Biostatistics and Oncology at the Johns Hopkins Bloomberg School of Public Health. His research focuses on the intersection of high dimensional data analysis, genomics, and public health. He is the Co-Editor of the popular Simply Statistics Blog and Co-Director of the Johns Hopkins Specialization in Data Science the largest data science program in the world.

Made in the USA
Lexington, KY
06 January 2018